This book is a call to the body of Christ, not to chase gifts, platforms, or public displays of power, but to pursue the presence of the One who changes everything. It's a warning against leaning on what looks spiritual while neglecting the deeper call to holiness, character, and fruit. And it's a prophetic reminder that signs and wonders should follow the believer—not replace the foundation of love, humility, and relationship with Jesus.

If you're hungry for authenticity, purity, and the real power of God that flows from a surrendered life, then lean in. Let this book challenge you. Let it provoke you. Let it stir up something eternal in you.

Because what you're about to read may sound crazy to the world. But you'll know deep down—that's God.

—Caleb Ring
Senior Pastor, River Clermont Church

When I read this book, I didn't just see Pastor Juan's story—I saw my own. From the streets to the pulpit, from brokenness to hope, this is more than a book—it's a mirror for every person who's ever felt disqualified by their past. Pastor Juan reminds us that what looks crazy to the world is often exactly where God shows up the most. This book carries weight because he's really lived that life and can take you to his darkest moments and show you that's where God can shine the brightest. If you're struggling to believe that God would do it for you, then this is a must read.

—Rey Sandoval
Pastor, Rise Church

I highly recommend this amazing book. I think this book will transform the lives of believers who are walking in God's divine purpose. Many of us today, including myself, miss the providence of God, the signature of God, on our every season. I believe in my heart this book will help you understand how to have great discernment so as not to miss God's opportunities and blessings in your life. And remember: A lot of times when God does something, it's out of the box. This book has the perfect title, *That's Crazy—No, That's God*.

—JOHN RAMIREZ
EVANGELIST

That's Crazy—No, That's God is one of those books that makes you stop and reflect on just how big and faithful God really is. Page after page, I found myself encouraged, challenged, and reminded that what seems impossible to us is just the beginning for Him.

This book is a bold testament to what happens when you step out in faith—and I'm so glad you're holding it in your hands.

—ZEE
PASTOR; CHRISTIAN MUSIC ARTIST; AUTHOR,
WHEN DADS WIN

This book will stir your spirit and ignite a fresh hunger to see the supernatural power of God move in your everyday life. Pastor Juan writes with authenticity, clarity, and contagious passion. Each chapter is packed with biblical insight, practical wisdom, and stories that build your faith. Let these pages mark you with bold expectation and fresh fire for what God can do through a surrendered life!

—Matt Cruz
Evangelist

If you've ever thought, "That's crazy," when someone shares what God did in their life—this book is for you. Juan reminds us that the same God who does the "big miracles" is also present in the everyday, ordinary moments of our faith journey. *That's Crazy—No, That's God* is a fresh, honest, and encouraging read for anyone learning to trust that God still shows up—and often in the most unexpected ways.

—Mike Thakur
Entrepreneur; Author, *Mike Drop*

For a man who was radically transformed from a lifelong criminal to a sold-out Christ follower, *That's Crazy—No, That's God* is a rallying cry for our church and the simplest way we've found to express the awesome power of God we observe Pastor Juan walk in daily.

This book is a life-giving dive into the simple yet powerful ways he accesses the supernatural in every area of his life. I am fully confident that when you read, accept, and apply the wisdom within, you too will begin to experience a God-honoring, wonder-filled life that causes people watching you to declare, "That's crazy!"—to which you will be able to reply, "No, that's God!"

—Todd Holts
Teaching Pastor, Get Wrapped Church

Reading Juan Martinez's story challenged me in the best way. This book isn't just inspiring—it's a wake-up call. Juan writes with such honesty and faith that you can't help but reflect on your own walk with God. His journey is full of moments that look wild to the world, but they're clearly the result of obedience and God's power at work.

What I appreciated most was how grounded everything is in Scripture. It's not hype—it's truth, lived out. If you've ever wondered what it looks like to really trust God, this book shows you.

—Ricky Bakker
President and CEO,
PTL Television Network and Church 2414

This is more than a book—it's a faith-stirring declaration of what happens when ordinary people choose to trust an extraordinary God. As a pastor, I'm constantly reminding believers that God still moves in power today, and this book is living proof. With every story, you'll see the fingerprints of a faithful God who honors obedience and shows up in the most unexpected ways. It challenges the limits of our human understanding and invites us into a deeper walk of trust, surrender, and expectancy. I wholeheartedly recommend this book to anyone hungry to see God move in real and miraculous ways. Read it—and let your faith rise.

—Brian Jennings
Lead Pastor, Breakthrough Church

When my good friend Juan Martinez asked me to read his new book and write an endorsement, I felt compelled not simply to skim through but to read it diligently. As president and founder of Life Christian University, it is incumbent upon me to read a large number of books and doctoral dissertations. I found myself in a season of incredible time demands, but I was sure this book would be full of divine revelation, and I was certainly not disappointed.

In unfolding his understanding of how much our heavenly Father wants us to experience a supernatural walk with Him in our Christian life, Dr. Martinez has penned what I consider to be one of the best and most complete encyclopedias of genuine discipleship that I have ever read. As he unfolds the truths from God's Word that will help any believer live a truly transformed life, he explains a step-by-step process that answers deep theological questions in a way understandable to a broad majority of Christians.

I know you will be inspired, encouraged, and challenged by reading *That's Crazy—No, That's God*. But more than that, I fully expect that you will experience the "supernatural becoming a reality" in your life from this time forward.

—DOUGLAS J. WINGATE, PHD
PRESIDENT AND FOUNDER, LIFE CHRISTIAN UNIVERSITY

I've heard a lot of testimonies, but Juan's story is different. It's raw. It's real. It's a radical grace in motion. He doesn't just talk about transformation; he lives it. This book is a front-row seat to the miracle-working power of God. If you've ever wondered if God can use someone like you, let Juan's story be your answer. He's not just a changed man; he's a called man.

—MONDO DE LA VEGA
HOST, *THE MONDO SHOW*;
AUTHOR, *MY CRAZY LIFE*

The Bible is filled with stories of people whose lives were radically transformed by the grace and power of God. People whose identities, circumstances, and purpose were completely rewritten by divine intervention. In *That's Crazy—No That's God*, Pastor Juan Martinez reminds us that this isn't the exception. It's meant to be the norm for every believer. Drawing from his own incredible journey, Pastor Juan doesn't just offer a theory; he shares a living testimony of God's miraculous power still at work today.

Through bold faith, radical obedience, and a relentless pursuit of Jesus, he shows us that the supernatural life isn't reserved for a few. It's available to all of us. If you lean into the life-changing truths in this book, you too will discover that what may seem "crazy" to the world is actually God working in ways that are beyond imagination.

—Dr. Andrew Heard
Inspire Church Houston

JUAN **MARTINEZ**

THAT'S CRAZY—NO, THAT'S GOD by Juan Martinez
Published by Charisma House, an imprint of Charisma Media
1150 Greenwood Blvd., Lake Mary, Florida 32746

Copyright © 2025 by Juan Martinez. All rights reserved.

Unless otherwise noted, all scriptures are from The ESV® Bible (The Holy Bible, English Standard Version®), copyright © 2001 by Crossway, a publishing ministry of Good News Publishers. Used by permission. All rights reserved.

Scripture quotations marked AMPC are from the Amplified® Bible (AMPC), Copyright © 1954, 1958, 1962, 1964, 1965, 1987 by The Lockman Foundation. Used by permission. Lockman.org

Scripture quotations marked CSB have been taken from the Christian Standard Bible®, Copyright © 2017 by Holman Bible Publishers. Used by permission. Christian Standard Bible® and CSB® are federally registered trademarks of Holman Bible Publishers.

Scripture quotations marked CJB are from the Complete Jewish Bible, copyright © 1998 by David H. Stern. All rights reserved.

Scripture quotations marked KJV are from the King James Version of the Bible.

Scripture quotations marked MEV are from the Modern English Version. Copyright © 2014, 2024 by Military Bible Association. Used by permission. All rights reserved.

Scripture quotations marked NASB are taken from the (NASB®) New American Standard Bible®, Copyright © 1960, 1971, 1977, 1995 by The Lockman Foundation. Used by permission. All rights reserved. www.lockman.org

Scripture quotations marked NIV are taken from the Holy Bible, New International Version®, NIV®. Copyright © 1973, 1978, 1984, 2011 by Biblica, Inc.® Used by permission of

Zondervan. All rights reserved worldwide. www.zondervan.com. The "NIV" and "New International Version" are trademarks registered in the United States Patent and Trademark Office by Biblica, Inc.®

Scripture quotations marked NKJV are taken from the New King James Version®. Copyright © 1982 by Thomas Nelson. Used by permission. All rights reserved.

Scripture quotations marked NLT are taken from the *Holy Bible*, New Living Translation, copyright ©1996, 2004, 2015 by Tyndale House Foundation. Used by permission of Tyndale House Publishers, Carol Stream, Illinois 60188. All rights reserved.

While the author has made every effort to provide accurate, up-to-date source information at the time of publication, statistics and other data are constantly updated. Neither the publisher nor the author assumes any responsibility for errors or for changes that occur after publication. Further, the publisher and author do not have any control over and do not assume any responsibility for third-party websites or their content.

For more resources like this, visit MyCharismaShop.com and the author's website at JuanMartinez.tv.

Cataloging-in-Publication Data is on file with the Library of Congress.
International Standard Book Number: 978-1-63641-509-3
E-book ISBN: 978-1-63641-510-9

1 2025
Printed in the United States of America

Most Charisma Media products are available at special quantity discounts for bulk purchase for sales promotions, premiums, fund-raising, and educational needs. For details, call us at (407) 333-0600 or visit our website at charismamedia.com.

To Jesus—my Savior, Redeemer, and everything. I still can't believe I'm living this life. You truly make all things possible. I finally got the revelation that it's not crazy—it's You!

To my wife, Ruthy—my Baby Ruth. Thank you for being my anchor, my ride or die, and the one who has walked every crazy and God-filled moment with me.

To all the ones who are willing to look foolish for the sake of the gospel—the ones who step out in faith when it makes no sense...who pray bold prayers, take crazy risks, and love with reckless abandon...so that when the world says, "That's crazy," heaven responds,

"No...that's God."

This is for you.

Now to him who is able to do immeasurably more than all we ask or imagine, according to his power that is at work within us, to him be glory in the church and in Christ Jesus throughout all generations, for ever and ever! Amen.

—Ephesians 3:20–21, NIV

CONTENTS

Introduction..........................xvii

CHAPTER 1 Seeing the Supernatural 1
CHAPTER 2 Purpose and Plans 27
CHAPTER 3 Crazy Characters 45
CHAPTER 4 Impossible? Or Immeasurably More Than You Can Imagine? 57
CHAPTER 5 Move-a-Mountain Faith 73
CHAPTER 6 Water of the Word......................95
CHAPTER 7 The Power of Prayer 115
CHAPTER 8 The Help of the Holy Spirit 131
CHAPTER 9 Living a Life of Expectation............. 149
CHAPTER 10 Supernatural Salvation 171

Notes.................................179
Acknowledgments......................181
About the Author 183

INTRODUCTION

IF YOU HAD told me back in the days when I was dealing drugs that I would be a pastor one day, I would have said, "That's crazy!"—especially since I didn't even know what a pastor was. If you had said that I would be married to a wonderful, godly woman, with a family that is like a Hispanic Brady Bunch, I would have said, "That's crazy!" When I went to prison and was sharing a cell with members of the Aryan Brotherhood, if you had told me that one day I would be leading a ministry to set captives free—whether their captivity is physical, mental, emotional, or spiritual—I would have told you, "That's crazy!" When I was trying—and failing—to fill the void in my life with drugs, alcohol, sex, violence, money, and being a big shot, if you had told me that I would one day be filled with love, joy, peace, hope, kindness, and faith, I would have said, "That's crazy!"

When you know my story and understand where I came from and where I am now, you might say, "That's crazy!"

But I would say, "No, that's God!"

The whole "That's crazy! No, that's God!" thing started because there was a season of my life when my story was unfolding, and I recognized that it was all by the grace of God—all of it. These amazing things happened both to me and to others, and I would always say, "That's crazy, man." Then one day, the Lord told me, "No, that's Me. What you're calling crazy is Me. You're just doing things that are out of your comfort zone, so you think it's crazy, but the reality is it's how I originally intended it in My plan, the one that was perfect before the fall of man."

God's Ways Are Not Our Ways

Have you ever heard someone say, "That's crazy!" when you shared a dream, a vision, or a calling from God? Maybe you have even thought, "That's crazy!" yourself about something the Lord revealed to you. Perhaps you've shared a testimony of the supernatural at work in your life, and the response from others was, "That's crazy!" Just because something throws you for a loop doesn't mean it's crazy. Our human minds often struggle to grasp the ways of God because His plans can seem impossible or even irrational from our limited perspective. But what we may call crazy is often just the manifestation of God's extraordinary work in our lives, the manifestation of the supernatural.

Isaiah 55:8–9 says, "For my thoughts are not your thoughts, neither are your ways my ways, declares the Lord. For as the heavens are higher than the earth, so are my ways higher than your ways and my thoughts than your thoughts." As a follower of Christ, you must recognize that God's ways are higher than your ways, and His thoughts are higher than your thoughts. When God moves in your life, it is not always going to look like what you expect. In fact, it frequently doesn't look like what you expect. But that doesn't mean it's crazy. It just means that

Introduction

God, who is immeasurably more than our human minds can fathom, is at work in your life.

First Corinthians 1:25 says, "For the foolishness of God is wiser than men, and the weakness of God is stronger than men." God's instructions may not always make sense to you, but His plans are perfect. Your role is to trust and obey, even when others think it's crazy, even when others think it's foolishness. Sometimes God calls you to do things that others don't understand. He calls you to do things that are contrary to human logic. But what appears irrational, when done in obedience, may actually be an act of faith that leads to your deliverance. It may be an act of faith that leads to a miracle. Jesus told us that what is impossible with man is possible with God (Luke 18:27).

As a follower of Jesus, you need to accept the truth that God's ways are not your ways. You need to accept the truth of God's Word, not just in your head but in your heart. You need to understand what it means to die to yourself. You need to totally depend on God and be empowered by the Holy Spirit. Those are the things that activate the supernatural in your life. Everything is better in Christ, so understand that what people may call crazy is often a manifestation of God's extraordinary work and the Holy Spirit's power in your life.

Chasing Miracles or Chasing Jesus?

One big difference between Christianity and every other religion is that every other religion is dependent upon what you have to do to get closer to God. In Christianity everything is about what God has done and continues to do to get you closer to Him. Throughout the entirety of the Bible, in both the Old and New Testaments, we see God reaching out to us to reconcile us to Himself, to draw us close so that we can live an abundant life in His unmerited grace. What is unmerited grace? It is what God gave us in Jesus Christ before the beginning of time.

The Gospel of John says,

> In the beginning was the Word, and the Word was with God, and the Word was God. He was with God in the beginning. All things were created through him, and apart from him not one thing was created that has been created. In him was life, and that life was the light of men. That light shines in the darkness, and yet the darkness did not overcome it.
> —John 1:1–5, CSB

So where is Jesus in this? Jesus is the Word. "The Word became flesh and dwelt among us. We observed his glory, the glory as the one and only Son from the Father, full of grace and truth" (John 1:14, CSB).

God has been reaching out to us since creation. He gave us the amazing Garden of Eden where the first people, Adam and Eve, lived and walked with God. But mankind messed things up by stepping out from under God's grace and taking matters into our own hands. As a result, God sent Adam and Eve out of the garden.

But God never gave up reaching out to us. In fact, His plan to restore us to right relationship with Him was there in the very words He spoke to the serpent who deceived Eve: "I will put enmity between you and the woman, and between your offspring and her offspring; he shall bruise your head, and you shall bruise his heel" (Gen. 3:15). God already had a plan to send Jesus to die on the cross for our sins so that our relationship with Him could be restored to how He intended it to be—intimate and authentic—without the consequences of sin that separated us from a holy God.

God wants to have an authentic relationship with you. You are His child. He loves you. I think one reason many believers are missing out on the supernatural in their lives is that they are not in an authentic relationship with their Creator. Instead of pursuing intimacy with God and getting to know His will and His ways, they are chasing the wrong things. They are chasing events. They are chasing experiences. They are chasing goose bumps. They are chasing signs and wonders. They are chasing miracles. But if you truly want to experience the supernatural in your life, you need to be chasing Jesus. When you chase Jesus, the supernatural follows you.

The supernatural is a by-product of relationship. It is a by-product of intimacy with the Lord. When you are pursuing a relationship with Jesus, the supernatural happens naturally. And Jesus wants a relationship with you. That is worth repeating. Jesus wants a relationship with *you*. He wants you to spend time in His presence. He wants you to spend time getting to know Him through worship, through prayer, and through reading His Word. He doesn't want a casual, surface-level relationship with you, as if you were just an acquaintance. He doesn't want a Sunday-morning-only relationship. He wants a deep, authentic, heart-level, everyday relationship with you.

In John 15:15 Jesus told His disciples, "No longer do I call you servants, for the servant does not know what his master is doing; but I have called you friends, for all that I have heard from my Father I have made known to you." Jesus wants a friendship with you. The Creator of the universe wants to be your friend. And He doesn't want the kind of friendship where you just say hi to each other when you happen to cross paths. He wants the kind of friendship where you know each other's hearts.

Obviously, Jesus knows your heart because He knows everything. But the question is, Do you know His heart? You may come to the Lord and ask Him for new tires for your car because with your limited perspective new tires seem like the biggest issue in your life. But I imagine God is thinking, "Is that all you want? Tires? I already knew about the tires. But I want to share My heart with you. I want to tell you what is going on in heaven right now. Do you want that too?"

Jesus said, "All that I have heard from my Father I have made known to you." Jesus wants to reveal the heart of the Father to you. He wants to reveal the love of the Father to you. He wants to reveal the will and the ways of the Father to you. He wants to reveal the plans and purposes and promises and perspective of the Father to you. That's the beauty of having a deep, meaningful relationship with God. But you can't get to know someone's heart if you never spend time with them, talking to them and getting to know their thoughts and their feelings and the things that move them.

If you have been chasing miracles instead of chasing Jesus, you need to know the truth. The truth is that signs and wonders always follow the believer. When you're submitted to the Word of God, accepting that it has final authority in your life, when you are living by faith, when you are being led by the Spirit, signs and wonders will follow—so much so that you will be the sign that will make people wonder.

Introduction

An aspiring artist once decided to leave a lucrative career to pursue painting full-time, even though he had never been formally trained. People thought it was a foolish decision, especially since the art world is notoriously competitive. Yet years later, the artist's work was celebrated globally, and his story became an inspiration to many. This mirrors the kind of faith that produces the supernatural in your life. It mirrors the kind of faith that trusts in God's promises, even when it seems impossible that those promises will be fulfilled. It is the kind of "crazy" faith that you are called to as a child of God.

God doesn't just do the unexpected—He delights in doing the impossible. Sometimes what seems chaotic or illogical is God creating something new in your life.

> Behold, I am doing a new thing; now it springs forth, do you not perceive it? I will make a way in the wilderness and rivers in the desert.
> —ISAIAH 43:19

When God calls you to something that seems crazy, you need to remember that it's not crazy; it's God. His plans may defy human logic, but they are always rooted in His love, wisdom, and power. God's calling in your life may seem risky or unwise by worldly standards, but He sees the full picture and leads you to success according to His will, His way, and His timing. Trust in Him, follow His lead, and watch as He does the impossible in your life.

So the next time you hear someone say, "That's crazy!" about what God is doing in your life, respond, "No, that's God."

Chapter 1
SEEING THE SUPERNATURAL

SUPERNATURAL FAITH BELIEVES that God can do the impossible. But there is a tension between faith and sight. There is a tension between divine power and human logic. There is a tension between revelation and reason.

Supernatural faith is based on revelation and trust in God's Word. First Corinthians 2:14 says, "The natural person does not accept the things of the Spirit of God, for they are folly to him, and he is not able to understand them because they are spiritually discerned." There is always that tension between the natural and the things of the Spirit of God. Without the understanding given to you by the Holy Spirit living in you, you won't recognize or understand the supernatural at work in your life. But when you have the Holy Spirit, He gives you the ability to discern the supernatural, to discern the power of God at work in your life and in the world.

The apostle Paul wrote about the tension between worldly wisdom and true wisdom:

> For the word of the cross is folly to those who are perishing, but to us who are being saved it is the power of God. For it is written, "I will destroy the wisdom of the wise, and the discernment of the discerning I will thwart."

> Where is the one who is wise? Where is the scribe? Where is the debater of this age? Has not God made foolish the wisdom of the world? For since, in the wisdom of God, the world did not know God through wisdom, it pleased God through the folly of what we preach to save those who believe. For Jews demand signs and Greeks seek wisdom, but we preach Christ crucified, a stumbling block to Jews and folly to Gentiles, but to those who are called, both Jews and Greeks, Christ the power of God and the wisdom of God. For the foolishness of God is wiser than men, and the weakness of God is stronger than men....
>
> But God chose what is foolish in the world to shame the wise; God chose what is weak in the world to shame the strong.
>
> —1 Corinthians 1:18–25, 27

That tension between worldly wisdom and true wisdom often causes people to walk in fear and by sight rather than walking by faith. There is a pull between fear and trust. But when you trust and keep your eyes on Jesus, you can step out of the boat and walk on the water, just like Peter did.

When you walk by sight, you allow fear of the enemy into your life. You're not living by faith; you're living in fear. But the fear of the enemy doesn't bring wisdom. The enemy is always going to try to talk you out of living by faith. He wants you to trust in human understanding and logic. He wants you to think what God is asking you to do really is crazy so that you delay your obedience or even flat out disobey. When you choose to buy into the lies of the enemy, you will be living in bondage rather than in the freedom and abundance God wants for you.

Remember, "the fear of the LORD is the beginning of wisdom" (Prov. 9:10, CSB). When you fear the Lord instead of the enemy, when you trust in the Lord with all your heart, when you choose to be God-dependent rather than self-reliant, the Holy Spirit will open your eyes, your mind, your heart, and your spirit to the supernatural at work all around you. "Not by might, nor by power, but by my Spirit, says the LORD of hosts" (Zech. 4:6).

CHANGE YOUR PERSPECTIVE

What do you think about when you hear the word *supernatural*? What do you think about when you hear the word *miracle*? What do you think about when you hear *signs and wonders*? Perhaps you think about someone getting up out of a wheelchair and taking off running. Perhaps you think about someone being delivered from a demon that has been tormenting them and stealing, killing, and destroying all that is good in their life. Perhaps you think about someone being set free from a crack addiction or a pornography addiction.

Without a doubt, all those things are supernatural. They are miracles. They are signs and wonders that can strengthen your faith and make you long for the supernatural to be at work in your life too.

But what if the supernatural is already at work in your life, but you just haven't noticed it? What if God has been working miracles in your life on a daily basis, but you don't recognize them because they are not what you expect? What if you don't see the signs and wonders in your life because you aren't looking with spiritual eyes?

Here's some truth: When you have peace even in the midst of a storm, that's supernatural.

When you have hope even when your circumstances and the devil are telling you that your situation is hopeless, that's supernatural.

When you overcome fear and share your faith, that's supernatural.

When you reach out with kindness to your enemy or a stranger, that's supernatural.

When the enemy of your soul is attacking you from every side and everything seems like it is going wrong but you still have joy—that's supernatural.

Second Corinthians 5:7 says, "For we walk by faith, not by sight." We don't walk by our limited human perspective and understanding. Human perception is finite, it's limited, and it's often clouded by fear, doubt, and worldly values. When you depend on your limited human perspective and understanding, it leads to anxiety and worry. It leads to being indecisive. It leads to a focus on temporary matters rather than eternal matters, the matters of the kingdom of God. That's why even in the midst of storms and sorrows, tests and trials, you need to be chasing Jesus, "the founder and perfecter of our faith, who for the joy that was set before him endured the cross, despising the shame, and is seated at the right hand of the throne of God" (Heb. 12:2). The trials of life build your faith:

> Consider it a great joy, my brothers and sisters, whenever you experience various trials, because you know that the testing of your faith produces

endurance. And let endurance have its full effect, so that you may be mature and complete, lacking nothing.

—James 1:2–4, csb

I am blessed to pastor an amazing church. But then when I'm on the road, I kick on as an evangelist. I prophesy. It's like a completely different world. I get so excited. It blesses me. I cry sometimes because I am so moved and humbled by the goodness of God. I'm still in awe that God would use me to say something specific to someone I've never met before. And I know without a doubt it's God. And they know without a doubt it's God, so they start crying.

Then I come back, and I'm a pastor again. And I think, "Ooh, I want to do it again!" because I love those moments when God uses me to evangelize or prophesy. But I have learned to recognize that just because I'm not prophesying does not mean God isn't working. I have learned not to minimize what God is doing. God works supernaturally just as much through a pastor or a teacher as through a prophet or an evangelist. When I'm teaching on Sunday morning and the Word of God convicts someone's heart, that's supernatural. When the care I give my flock softens someone's heart, that's God.

The experience of God doesn't always lead to belief. The experience of the supernatural doesn't necessarily lead to faith. There are many people who have witnessed signs and wonders, but their hearts are still far from God. It happened over and over again in the Bible with the children of Israel, and it still happens today. That's why we need spirit and truth. That's why we need pastors who are operating supernaturally to teach their flocks, guard their flocks, feed their flocks, and love their flocks. The truth is that a pastor who only prophesied to his church would not be very loving—and the church would lack the solid foundation of the truth of the Word of God. So even though a pastor teaching the Word of God may seem unexciting and mundane, the truth is that it is supernatural, if for no other reason than that God promises, "So my word that comes from my mouth will not return to me empty, but it will accomplish what I please and will prosper in what I send it to do" (Isa. 55:11, CSB).

God moves how He wants to move. He says what He wants to say when He wants to say it and how He wants to say it. We have to stop making God this cookie-cutter thing, thinking we can make the supernatural happen the way we want. We can't manufacture a move of God. I might prophesy today, but that does not mean I will prophesy tomorrow. We need to be sensitive to the moving of the Holy Spirit. We need to recognize that the supernatural is more than just the "crazy" stuff. We need to change our perspective and recognize that the supernatural happens all the time in both big ways and small ways.

SPIRIT AND TRUTH

The Lord wants worshippers, people who posture their hearts in a place to love Him, to accept His Word, and to be obedient. Jesus told the woman at the well, "But the hour is coming, and is now here, when the true worshipers will worship the Father in spirit and truth, for the Father is seeking such people to worship him. God is spirit, and those who worship him must worship in spirit and truth" (John 4:23–24).

Seeing the Supernatural

What is a worshipper? What does it mean to worship? *Merriam-Webster* defines *worship* as "to honor or show reverence for as a divine being or supernatural power; to regard with great or extravagant respect, honor, or devotion."[1] Although that is a good start, there is more to it than that.

In biblical scholarship and interpretation there is something called the law of first mention. It means that the first mention of a word, concept, or doctrine in the Bible provides the foundation of the understanding of that word, concept, or doctrine. The first time *worship* is mentioned in the Bible is when God asked Abraham to sacrifice Isaac:

> After these things God tested Abraham and said to him, "Abraham!" And he said, "Here I am." He said, "Take your son, your only son Isaac, whom you love, and go to the land of Moriah, and offer him there as a burnt offering on one of the mountains of which I shall tell you." So Abraham rose early in the morning, saddled his donkey, and took two of his young men with him, and his son Isaac. And he cut the wood for the burnt offering and arose and went to the place of which God had told him. On the third day Abraham lifted up his eyes and saw the place from afar. Then Abraham said to his young men, "Stay here with the donkey; I and the boy will go over there and *worship* and come again to you."
> —GENESIS 22:1–5, EMPHASIS ADDED

The first act of worship was an act of obedience. God asked Abraham to do something contrary to human logic. God asked Abraham to do something that we would call crazy. Yet in an act of worship, Abraham obeyed.

The first act of worship was also an act of faith. Abraham

knew what God had promised him. God had promised that his offspring would outnumber the stars (Gen. 15:5). God promised He would multiply Abraham greatly, saying, "I have made you the father of a multitude of nations. I will make you exceedingly fruitful, and I will make you into nations, and kings shall come from you. And I will establish my covenant between me and you and your offspring after you throughout their generations for an everlasting covenant, to be God to you and to your offspring after you" (Gen. 17:5–7). And God also specifically said He would establish His covenant with Isaac (Gen. 17:21). So when God asked Abraham to offer Isaac on the altar, Abraham obeyed and demonstrated supernatural faith. Abraham knew that Isaac was the heir to the covenant, which is why he said, "I and the boy will…come again to you" (Gen. 22:5). Abraham knew that if he sacrificed Isaac, God would raise him from the dead in order to keep His covenant:

> By faith Abraham, when he was tested, offered up Isaac, and he who had received the promises was in the act of offering up his only son, of whom it was said, "Through Isaac shall your offspring be named." He considered that God was able even to raise him from the dead, from which, figuratively speaking, he did receive him back.
> —Hebrews 11:17–19

A heart postured to worship is both obedient and full of faith.

Worship isn't just singing. Remember, God is looking for worshippers who will worship Him in spirit *and* in truth. You can be singing and praising your heart out, but if you go live like God hasn't done anything in your life and you're no different from anyone in the world, you aren't worshipping in spirit and in truth. It has been said that obedience is the highest form of worship. First Samuel 15:22 says, "Has the LORD as great delight in burnt offerings and sacrifices, as in obeying the voice of the LORD? Behold, to obey is better than sacrifice, and to listen than the fat of rams."

The Hebrew word for *worship* means to bow down, to fall down, to prostrate oneself, and to pay homage. But it also means to submit oneself.[2] True worship involves submitting to the Lord. It involves obeying Him and His Word. You are just worshipping in spirit when you lift your voice to the Lord on Sunday morning but then live however you want to live the rest of the week, regardless of the consequences for you and for other people.

I feel like lot of people think things like, "Why is it a big deal that I'm living with my girlfriend? Everybody does it," "Why does it matter if I cheat on my taxes?" "Why shouldn't I get drunk every weekend?" "Why can't I lie to my boss? What's the big deal?" They don't understand that the reason God gave us boundaries is because He loves us. That is a fact. If you are a parent, I'm sure you understand the concept. You give your children boundaries to protect them, to keep them safe, to help them grow, and to help them learn, and you do it out of love. God is a good Father, and He gives you boundaries to protect you, to keep you safe, to help you grow, and to help you learn, and He does it out of love.

People have misrepresented life with Jesus. Sometimes we look at the Bible as a big book of rules, rules, and more rules with the intentions of keeping you bound up and keeping you from enjoying life. People think that once they start following Jesus, their lives will be over. But it's totally the opposite of that. My life right now is better than it has ever been. The Bible provides boundaries so you can live in freedom without all the baggage and consequences of sin. God is a loving Father who wants to protect you from yourself and the world. For example, He doesn't want you to have to deal with the consequences of sexually transmitted diseases, having babies out of wedlock, harmful soul ties, rejection, heartbreak, destroyed marriage covenants, and broken families, which is why He designed sex to occur only within a marriage between a man and a woman. When you go outside that boundary, it is harmful—both to you and to others. When you have sex, you become one flesh with the other person, so if you don't have the protection of the marriage covenant, you are going to end up with part of yourself being ripped out. So God doesn't tell you to not have sex with anyone other than your spouse because He doesn't want you to enjoy yourself; it's because He loves you, and He doesn't want you (or any of the others affected by your sin) to get hurt.

Worshipping your heart out on Sunday is great. But what does your life look like the rest of the week? When you worship, are you worshipping in spirit and truth? Will you live according to what feels good or what seems right or what the world says is the way to go, or will you move in the promises of God?

You have the Word of God in you when you are reading it, writing it on your heart, and meditating on it to grow as a believer. Do you have that truth element in your worship? You cannot remove it and still be worshipping in spirit and in truth. As part of developing an authentic relationship with Jesus, I'm feeding on the Word. I'm meditating on the Word. I'm thinking about it. And my meditation on the Word colors my worship. It affects the way I see God, the way I praise Him, my understanding of His character, my understanding of His goodness, and the reasons I have to worship Him.

You can't have faith without the Word. It's just impossible. Romans 10:17 says, "So faith comes from hearing, and hearing through the word of Christ." And it's impossible to apply the Word without the Spirit. You need the Word and the Spirit. You need to worship in spirit and in truth. You need both sides—there needs to be a balance.

There are people and churches who are completely grounded in the Word, which is awesome, but they are super dry because they lack the oil of the Spirit. They have the Word without much of the Spirit, so they never live out the Word in a supernatural way. When you have the Word without the Spirit, it can lead to legalism.

Then, you have the people who are so full of the Spirit that they want to hop around all day, which is awesome, but it doesn't do any good if it's not leading them into truth. They want goose bumps, but they don't want sanctification. When you have the Spirit without much of the Word, you lack foundation, and it can lead to false teaching, heresy, or apostasy.

Beyond that who cares if you're talking in tongues all day but not edifying anyone? What is the benefit of operating in the gifts of the Spirit if you don't have fruit, such as a good marriage, healthy relationships, peace, love, and joy? In 1 Corinthians when the apostle Paul taught about spiritual gifts, he said to desire the gifts. Then he immediately said, "I will show you a still more excellent way" (1 Cor. 12:31). And he began to talk about love. He was saying the gifts don't mean anything if you aren't operating in love:

> If I speak in the tongues of men and of angels, but have not love, I am a noisy gong or a clanging cymbal. And if I have prophetic powers, and understand all mysteries and all knowledge, and if I have all faith, so as to remove mountains, but have not love, I am nothing. If I give away all I have, and if I deliver up my body to be burned, but have not love, I gain nothing.
> —1 Corinthians 13:1–3

We are to "pursue love, and earnestly desire the spiritual gifts" (1 Cor. 14:1). The gifts are "the manifestation of the Spirit for the common good" (1 Cor. 12:7), but the common good won't happen if the gifts aren't being used in love and on a solid foundation of the truth of the Word of God.

We are living in a generation when a lot of people are not reading their Bibles. They are getting their knowledge of the Word, the kingdom of God, and the things of the Spirit from Facebook reels, Instagram posts, TikToks, and YouTube videos. The problem is that the reel isn't always real. The posts may be pointing you in the wrong direction, but you won't know that if you don't have the Word of God in your heart and mind. The Word of God has to have authority in your life. In fact, God's Word should have final authority in your everyday decisions. If you remove God's Word, then you don't have truth. When you don't have truth, you only have spirit, and it's going to look super weird.

And please don't dismiss the danger of falling into false doctrine, or even falling away from the faith, when you don't know the truth. You can't recognize the lies of the enemy if you don't know what the truth is. That is dangerous. The enemy comes to steal, kill, and destroy (John 10:10). If you don't have the Word, you don't have a weapon to fight the enemy. The Word of God is the sword of the Spirit, and it is the only weapon in our spiritual armor (Eph. 6:17). And don't forget that since "faith comes from hearing, and hearing through the word of Christ" (Rom. 10:17), without the Word of God you don't have "the shield of faith, with which you can extinguish all the flaming darts of the evil one" (Eph. 6:16). Don't let the enemy lead you away from the Lord and back into bondage because you don't know the truth.

Remember, "true worshipers will worship the Father in spirit and truth, for the Father is seeking such people to worship him" (John 4:23). You need the balance between spirit and truth. You need the balance between the Word and the Spirit. That is the kind of worship God is looking for. He is looking for worship that is an act of obedience. He is seeking worship that is an act of faith.

And one more thing—God is seeking worship that is an act of love. The Greek word for *worship* literally means to kiss or to kiss the hand toward.[3] Worship is like blowing kisses to Jesus. It is an act of love for the One who saved you, redeemed you, chose you, forgave you, calls you by name, sees you, loves you, accepts you, protects you, provides for you, and blesses you. He is worthy of your love. He is worthy of your worship.

THE ATTACK ON COVENANT

God is faithful. He doesn't just make promises. He makes what is called a covenant. A covenant is a relationship between two partners who make binding promises to each other and work together to reach a common goal.

The concept of *covenant* has been lost in modern society. Promises are broken when new circumstances arise. Contracts are broken, and one party simply shrugs and says, "Sue me." Marriage is supposed to be a covenant between a man and a woman for life, but divorce is commonplace today, even in the church.

We are good at blaming the world for everything that is going wrong within covenantal relationships, but that is just a symptom of the attack on covenants. The devil wants you to blame anyone and everyone rather than taking responsibility for your own actions—the more you blame others, the easier it is to forsake a covenant.

I believe the attack on covenants is one of the reasons we miss out on seeing the supernatural at work.

To keep covenants strong, we need to take responsibility for our own actions and work together to show the world the power of covenant.

That means I can't blame the world if my marriage is struggling. It's my responsibility to love my wife the way "Christ loved the church and gave himself up for her" (Eph. 5:25). It's my responsibility to show the world what Jesus can do in my marriage and in my family. It is also my responsibility to show the world how powerful covenants are in the way I treat my friends, the way I handle contracts, and the way I do business. It is my responsibility to be faithful to the covenants I have committed to.

Regardless of how unfaithful people may be, God will never be unfaithful to His covenant promises. Faithfulness is part of God's character. Deuteronomy 7:9 says, "Know that the LORD your God is God, the faithful God who keeps his gracious covenant loyalty for a thousand generations with those who love him and keep his commands" (CSB).

You have to understand that when you are in authentic relationship with God, you start receiving His faithfulness. Then when you start moving in faith, you get to reproduce that faithfulness in your relationships with other people. There is an overflow of the faithfulness of God from you to the people in your life.

When I think about the attack on marriages, I realize the first human covenant God instituted is the one we tend to put last. Society has devalued marriage, and even believers are falling for the enemy's lies. Oh, we may be good at putting on marriage conferences, which can be helpful, but I think we stink at counteracting the impact of the world, taking back our territory from the enemy and advancing into his territory, and doing all the things we need to do to experience the supernatural in the two becoming one.

God started human covenants with marriage: "Therefore a man shall leave his father and his mother and hold fast to his wife, and they shall become one flesh" (Gen. 2:24). Fast-forward to Ephesians, and the Word of God basically says that if you want to have a strong church, you need to look at the marriage:

> Wives, submit to your own husbands, as to the Lord. For the husband is the head of the wife even as Christ is the head of the church, his body, and is himself its Savior. Now as the church submits to Christ, so also wives should submit in everything to their husbands.
>
> Husbands, love your wives, as Christ loved the

> church and gave himself up for her, that he might sanctify her, having cleansed her by the washing of water with the word, so that he might present the church to himself in splendor, without spot or wrinkle or any such thing, that she might be holy and without blemish. In the same way husbands should love their wives as their own bodies. He who loves his wife loves himself. For no one ever hated his own flesh, but nourishes and cherishes it, just as Christ does the church, because we are members of his body. "Therefore a man shall leave his father and mother and hold fast to his wife, and the two shall become one flesh." This mystery is profound, and I am saying that it refers to Christ and the church. However, let each one of you love his wife as himself, and let the wife see that she respects her husband.
> —Ephesians 5:22–33

The apostle Paul was talking about marriage, but he was talking about the relationship between Jesus and the church at the same time. We won't have a strong church until we can institute the gospel in strong marriages. When you see a truly strong marriage, it's because two people have accepted Jesus as Lord and Savior, and they are bringing the overflow of the faithfulness of God into their marriage. That's a strong marriage. And when there is a strong marriage, there are two strong people. The secret to a strong marriage is right there in Ephesians. Paul called it a mystery. And do you know what that means? It means a strong marriage is supernatural. Don't miss out on seeing that!

We need to get back to focusing on strengthening—or, if needed, restoring and rebuilding—covenant relationships, starting with marriage. Strong marriages are foundational.

Without strong marriages families fall apart. And the more families fall apart, the more the church starts to fall apart too. Without a solid foundation, starting in the home, we will never have a powerful, supernatural church.

I'm passionate about this. I'm tearing up thinking about this. The sad truth is we would often rather see a miraculous healing than a strong marriage. I'm not knocking blind eyes being opened. I'm not knocking the lame walking. God still does those things, and they are supernatural. But we need to be chasing Jesus rather than chasing miracles. We need to be building solid foundations of truth—in our churches, in our families, in our marriages, and in ourselves. And if we remove the foundation of a covenant marriage, and we remove the foundation of Jesus Christ, the enemy can and will come to steal, kill, and destroy.

If you want to see the supernatural, you need to fight back against the devil's attack on covenants. And it starts with your relationship with Jesus. The relationship between Christ and the church is a marriage, and in a marriage the two become one. So that's where you begin—becoming one with Jesus.

Living in the Power and Authority of the Spirit

If you want to see the supernatural happening in your life and in the world around you, you need to live in the power and authority of the Holy Spirit. That means saying no to your flesh. The Word of God says, "For those who live according to the flesh set their minds on the things of the flesh, but those who live according to the Spirit set their minds on the things of the Spirit. For to set the mind on the flesh is death, but to set the mind on the Spirit is life and peace" (Rom. 8:5–6). When the flesh dies, the spirit lives. Every no to the flesh is a yes to a promise. Every time you say no to your flesh, you are sowing seeds of life, freedom, and peace.

There is a conflict between the flesh and the Spirit in us all: "For the desires of the flesh are against the Spirit, and the desires of the Spirit are against the flesh, for these are opposed to each other, to keep you from doing the things you want to do" (Gal. 5:17). To walk in the power of the Holy Spirit, you have to die to yourself—putting off the old man, putting on the new man (new creation), being changed into the image of Christ from glory to glory, and being transformed by the renewing of your mind:

> I have been crucified with Christ. It is no longer I who live, but Christ who lives in me. And the life I now live in the flesh I live by faith in the Son of God, who loved me and gave himself for me.
> —GALATIANS 2:20

> …to put off your old self, which belongs to your former manner of life and is corrupt through deceitful desires, and to be renewed in the spirit of your minds, and to put on the new self, created after the likeness of God in true righteousness and holiness.
> —EPHESIANS 4:22–24

> Therefore, if anyone is in Christ, he is a new creation. The old has passed away; behold, the new has come.
> —2 CORINTHIANS 5:17

> We all, with unveiled faces, are looking as in a mirror at the glory of the Lord and are being transformed into the same image from glory to glory; this is from the Lord who is the Spirit.
> —2 CORINTHIANS 3:18, CSB

> Do not be conformed to this age, but be transformed by the renewing of your mind, so that you may discern what is the good, pleasing, and perfect will of God.
> —ROMANS 12:2, CSB

There are people who try to do the Christian life without Christ, without the Holy Spirit. They want heaven, they want the supernatural, they want the miraculous, but they are still living a worldly life. When you are in the world, your flesh leads your body and your mind. You do whatever your flesh tells you to do. It doesn't matter. You just do it. Then you get saved, and there should be a change. When you are in Christ, you're supposed to be feeding your spirit man rather than your flesh.

As a follower of Christ you allow your spirit man to take authority over what your mind or your flesh wants to do. You train your mind and body to let the Word of God have the final authority. You do this by the power of the Spirit. You do this by being led by the Spirit. You allow the Spirit to lead you into all truth. Jesus said, "When the Spirit of truth comes, he will guide you into all the truth" (John 16:13). But you have to choose to let the Holy Spirit lead you. You have to choose to die to yourself: "If anyone wants to follow after me, let him deny himself, take up his cross daily, and follow me" (Luke 9:23, CSB). When you are living in the power of the Spirit, your spirit man is telling your mind and body what to do.

On the flip side, when you are a carnal Christian, you are living a powerless life. The apostle Paul spoke of people "having the appearance of godliness, but denying its power" (2 Tim. 3:5). Carnal Christians are like that. Everything may look fine on the outside, but they are living without the power of the Holy Spirit to help them, comfort them, transform them, counsel them, and guide them. Rather than being led by the Spirit, they are being led by their flesh. They are being led by their feelings. They are letting their thoughts and opinions—regardless of whether they are based on truth—lead their spirit man.

If you want to live in the power of the Spirit, there has to be an end to your way. When you accept God's way and live accordingly, you are led by the power of the Spirit. God's way may seem crazy to your natural man but is the only way that leads to life, freedom, peace, joy, and all the other abundant blessings God has for you. It is the way that leads to the supernatural. Jesus said, "I am the way" (John 14:6). God's ways are not ours (Isa. 55:8). And when you are being led by the power of the Spirit, "your ears shall hear a word behind you, saying, 'This is the way, walk in it,' when you turn to the right or when you turn to the left" (Isa. 30:21).

With the power of the Spirit comes the authority of the Spirit. I think of authority this way: Say a guy jumps out in the middle of the road and yells at you to stop your car. If the guy is wearing a uniform from a fast-food restaurant, you are probably going to just swerve around him and keep going. But if the guy is wearing a police officer's uniform and flashing a badge, you are going to slam on the brakes. The difference between the two guys is that one has authority because of his position.

A police officer has inherent authority, but it's your choice whether you submit to that authority. However, choosing to not submit to that authority has consequences—you might even end up in prison.

The Holy Spirit has inherent authority too, as does the Word of God. And just like with the police officer, you get to choose whether to submit to that authority. And just like not submitting to the authority of law enforcement can land you in prison, not submitting to the authority of the Spirit and the Word of God can land you in prison, whether physical, emotional, mental, or spiritual.

When the authority of the Spirit comes, it means that God's Word has the final say. When God tells you something, you may not like it. You may be a little afraid. You may not understand. It may be pushing you out of your comfort zone. But the Word of God has authority. It is *the* final authority. Remember, victory happens the moment you die to yourself.

When you are living in the power and authority of the Spirit, you are moving in the authority the Word has over your life, and you are moving in the power of the Spirit toward the great truth. When you do that enough, it starts to come naturally. And you don't have to look weird doing it. In all honesty there are times it may look a little wild, but it's not weird.

When Jesus walked the earth as a man, He did only what the Father said. Jesus said it over and over again:

> My food is to do the will of him who sent me and to accomplish his work.
> —JOHN 4:34

> I seek not my own will but the will of him who sent me.
>
> —John 5:30

> For I have come down from heaven, not to do my own will but the will of him who sent me.
>
> —John 6:38

Jesus' purpose was to do the will of the Father, even when it seemed to defy human logic. When Jesus was praying in the garden before His crucifixion, He was praying so earnestly that He was sweating blood (Luke 22:44). Jesus was flesh and blood, just like us, and His flesh was warring against the Spirit. He prayed, "My Father, if it be possible, let this cup pass from me; nevertheless, not as I will, but as you will" (Matt. 26:39). Jesus didn't want to be crucified, but He was living in the power and authority of the Spirit, so He moved in the direction of the will of the Father. Jesus was submitted to the will of God.

Submission to the will and Word of God leads to freedom. It leads to abundant life. When you live in the power and authority of the Spirit, when you allow the Holy Spirit to lead you, you will see the supernatural.

When I got saved in prison, I intended to pray for people throughout the prison. But don't you know that I didn't pray for anyone at first. My flesh was getting in the way of the Spirit. There was this table where a bunch of gang members sat. I remember thinking, "I ain't going over there!" But that was what God wanted me to do.

So I went over to the table. I had a piece of paper and a pen. I said, "Guys, I know you are all going through something. I'm going to church, so I wanted to know if you guys wanted me to pray for anything." I put the paper and pen down so they could write down their prayer requests. Then I took the paper, went to church in the prison, and prayed for people. One guy had written that he wanted to get to know his daughter. I prayed for him, and one day he said, "Hey, I got a visit from my daughter." I saw other answers to prayer too. I saw the supernatural—sometimes in big things and sometimes in small things—because I was living in the power and authority of the Spirit.

I became hungry to see the Spirit move. Some people might say I was crazy to talk to a bunch of gang members, but it wasn't crazy. It was God. And if I hadn't stepped out with faith in the power and authority of the Spirit, I would have missed out on seeing God's Word work in somebody else's life. So I'm going to choose the Spirit above what I think, above my opinion.

I have a funny story from early in my ministry about walking in the power and authority of the Spirit. I went to minister in Breckenridge, Texas. I got a little cocky and said, "Lord, bring me someone in a wheelchair. I'm gonna stand them up today." So there it was. I said it. And the Lord provided a guy in a wheelchair. But I did not get him up. I chickened out. I put a hand on his shoulder and said, "Lord, I pray for his heart." It was just a casual prayer. I felt so discouraged, so when I walked away, I prayed, "Man, God, I'm discouraged."

He told me, "It's never you that is standing them up, and you are way too cocky and prideful." The Lord was right of course. I messed up. My flesh had gotten in the way of the Spirit. But here's the deal: God looks at the heart. He's not like people that look only at the outward appearance. So even when you mess up—when you truly think God said something, but you misunderstood or misheard—God isn't going to stop working in your life. He isn't going to stop speaking to you. He isn't going to stop using you to advance the kingdom. He looks at your heart. He can take your mistake and use it for good, for "all things work together for the good of those who love God, who are called according to his purpose" (Rom. 8:28, CSB). And then because He loves you, God will teach you somewhere along the line to listen better.

That's what happened to me. I continued to chase Jesus. I continued to be good soil for the Word to bear fruit. I continued to say no to my flesh and yes to the promises of God. I learned to listen better, and I continued to be led by the Spirit.

Then about a year later I was preaching in a church in Palacios, Texas. I didn't go in with a cocky attitude. I wasn't acting out of pride. I was just doing what I do, living in the power and authority of the Spirit.

A guy using a walker came in. I heard the Lord say, "Grab his walker." I didn't think twice. I remember just pulling the walker away, but my wife says I threw it across the room. All that really matters is that walker was gone. The guy fell forward on me, holding on to my shoulders. I started jumping up and down, speaking what God was telling me to say. Then that guy let go of my shoulders and started running. The service started at ten in the morning and didn't end until three in the afternoon. That guy walked out with his walker on his shoulder. Since it was a small town, it wasn't long before everyone knew what had happened. I know there were a lot of people thinking and saying, "That's crazy!" But it wasn't crazy. It was God.

When I went to the service that day, I wasn't chasing

miracles. I wasn't thinking, "I'm gonna get somebody out of their walker." I was thinking about ministering the Word. I was thinking about giving people truth. I was being led by the Spirit of God. I believe that God was truly showing me the fruit of obedience when I live in the power and authority of the Spirit. God was showing me that He is the One who will get people out of wheelchairs and off of walkers. It's all about Him and His timing; it's never about me. That is a life lesson I have carried in my heart ever since.

Again, there is tension between human logic and faith. There is tension between the flesh and the Spirit. But when you change your perspective, when you have a balance of Word and Spirit, when you are living in the power and authority of the Spirit, you are going to see the supernatural. It may not look like what you expect—it may even seem crazy. But it's not crazy; it's God. And the more you see the supernatural, the more natural it will become.

Chapter 2
PURPOSE AND PLANS

So why does God move supernaturally? What is the purpose of miracles, signs, and wonders? Are the things we often call crazy part of God's plan?

First and foremost, everything is about God's glory. When Jesus heard that His friend Lazarus was sick, Jesus knew that Lazarus was going to die of his illness. But Jesus said, "This illness does not lead to death. It is for the glory of God, so that the Son of God may be glorified through it" (John 11:4). And Lazarus did die. But he didn't stay dead. Jesus arrived in Bethany—where Lazarus and his sisters, Mary and Martha, lived—four days after Lazarus died. It seemed like Jesus was too late. It seemed like there was no hope. But with God it's never too late. What looks like a dead end to us is just an opportunity for God to bring new life. We need to trust His timing, even when it feels crazy.

Since it had been four days, there was no doubt Lazarus was dead. In fact, when Jesus ordered the stone at the front of Lazarus' tomb to be moved away, Martha warned Him that it would stink because of how long Lazarus had been dead. Then Jesus said to Martha, "Did I not tell you that if you believed you would see the glory of God?" (John 11:40).

And that is exactly what happened. Jesus prayed, "Father, I thank you that you have heard me. I knew that you always hear me, but I said this on account of the people standing around, that they may believe that you sent me" (vv. 41–42).Then He called out in a loud voice, "Lazarus, come out" (v. 43). Lazarus, who had been dead four days, then walked out of his tomb. Lazarus wasn't a zombie or a ghost. He had been raised from the dead and restored to life. It was a miracle. It was supernatural. And the purpose was the glory of God.

The primary purpose of everything is the glory of God. First Corinthians 10:31 says, "Do all to the glory of God." But God's purpose goes beyond just His glory. Jesus said, "For this purpose I was born and for this purpose I have come into the world—to bear witness to the truth" (John 18:37). Think about all the things Jesus did when He came into the world. He healed the sick. He opened blind eyes. He made the lame walk. He raised people from the dead. He cast out demons. He walked on water, and He had Peter do the same. He prophesied. He interpreted the Scriptures in such a way that even when He was just a boy, the rabbis in the temple were "amazed at his understanding" (Luke 2:47). He turned water to wine. He multiplied bread and fish to feed thousands of people. He calmed storms.

All these miracles, signs, and wonders brought glory to God. But more than that, they testified to the truth. They testified that Jesus was and is and always will be the Son of God. They testified that He is the living Word of God. They testified that the written Word of God is true. They testified that God is a good Father who loves His children and longs for them to be restored to right relationship with Him. They testified that God is "merciful and gracious, slow to anger, and abounding in steadfast love and faithfulness, keeping steadfast love for thousands, forgiving iniquity and transgression and sin" (Exod. 34:6–7). They testified that Jesus is "the way, and the truth, and the life. No one comes to the Father except through [Him]" (John 14:6).

The Bible also says, "The reason the Son of God appeared was to destroy the works of the devil" (1 John 3:8). Jesus came to set us free from slavery to sin. He conquered death, hell, and the grave. First Corinthians 15:54–55 says, "Death is swallowed up in victory. O death, where is your victory? O death, where is your sting?" In the Book of Revelation, Jesus said, "I am the First and the Last, and the Living One. I was dead, but look—I am alive forever and ever, and I hold the keys of death and Hades" (1:17–18, CSB). It was prophesied all the way back in the Garden of Eden that Jesus would crush Satan's head (Gen. 3:15), and that is exactly what He did.

God doesn't do miracles just for the sake of doing miracles. Every supernatural act, big or small, brings God glory, testifies of the truth, and destroys the works of the devil.

THE SHORTCUT?

When I think about the supernatural, I always come back to faith. Faith pleases God. In fact, it's impossible to please God without faith. So when you move in faith, when you step out in faith, it pleases God.

The supernatural doesn't have to be someone getting out of a wheelchair. It could be the fruit of the Spirit operating in your life or the Holy Spirit helping you get rid of a mental stronghold like fear or condemnation. Changing your perspective so you recognize those things as supernatural helps build your faith. It also starts moving you to where God can use you to operate in things that require great faith. You can start small, but as you see God begin to act in response to your faith for little things, it will give you the ability to believe God for great things.

God responds to faith. He responds to expectation. But His responses don't always meet our expectations. God supernaturally intervenes in the natural, but it is often in a way we don't expect. God does not give cookie-cutter answers to prayer. And that builds our faith too.

The more I grow in Christ, the more I realize everything is about Jesus. Everything points to Jesus. Everything is about His plan and His purposes. The problem is that sometimes we mess up His plan by trying to add our own plans to it. But remember, God's thoughts are not our thoughts, nor are His ways our ways. We need to trust His plan, knowing that it is a good plan to give us hope and a future (Jer. 29:11).

We often add our plans and our answers to what God is saying without even thinking twice. "I got it, Lord. Let me do this." It's like we forget all that He saved us from, all the stupid stuff we got stuck in, all the messes we made. We think we got it, but we don't. Don't overcomplicate God's solution with your answer.

God always instructs. His instructions may not make sense to us, they may seem crazy when viewed with human logic, but His plan is perfect: "As for God, His way is perfect" (2 Sam. 22:31, NKJV). The Lord calls us to do things we don't understand, and He wants us to have faith and obey—and that will actually lead to our deliverance. God's plan of salvation works. God's plan of Jesus works.

Purpose and Plans

Why do we add so many things? Why do we live most of the time not trusting in the Lord with all our hearts? The reality is we want God to break it down before we move. We want Him to explain the plan so we can step out in knowledge rather than in faith.

It is especially hard to move in faith when you are suffering, when you are in a storm, when you are in a wilderness season. But God uses the wilderness season to develop your character in preparation for what's coming next.

We all face times in the wilderness. The children of Israel spent forty years in the wilderness. John the Baptist lived pretty much his whole life in the wilderness. Jesus was tempted in the wilderness after fasting for forty days. David spent time in the wilderness even though he was called a man after God's own heart. Elijah was a prophet who called down fire from heaven in a supernatural showdown on Mount Carmel and then immediately ended up in the wilderness.

Wilderness seasons happen. While you're in a wilderness season, you may be like the children of Israel, who complained and told the Lord, "We are just so sick of the manna." But the truth is that manna had 100 percent of the required daily nutrients for wandering in the wilderness. God provided everything the children of Israel needed. They may not have had the cucumbers, melons, and onions they had in Egypt, but when they were in Egypt, they were in bondage. (See Numbers 11.)

God uses the wilderness season to teach us, but the enemy uses the wilderness season to attack us. The enemy is the father of lies (John 8:44). He will come against you with his lies while you are in the wilderness: "Wasn't it better to be in bondage? You had onions!"

Don't fall for the enemy's lies! Jesus said, "The thief comes only to steal and kill and destroy. I came that they may have life and have it abundantly" (John 10:10). God wants you to have abundant life. When you are in a wilderness season, the enemy tries to break you because he wants to destroy you. But when God breaks you, it's not because He wants you broken. He is breaking you because He wants you whole. He breaks you to build you back up better. It's like in the military—they break you so they can build you back up into a soldier, not to destroy you.

God has a purpose for you, and the devil wants to steal that. He wants to destroy that. He wants to kill you if he can. Even the wilderness season has a purpose. When the children of Israel were preparing to enter the Promised Land, Moses told them,

> Go in and possess the land that the LORD swore to give to your fathers. And you shall remember the whole way that the LORD your God has led you these forty years in the wilderness, that he might humble you, testing you to know what was in your heart, whether you would keep his commandments or not. And he humbled you and let you hunger and fed you with manna, which you did not know, nor did your fathers know, that he might make you know that man does not live by bread alone, but man lives by every word that comes from the mouth of the LORD. Your clothing did not wear out on you and your foot did not swell these forty years. Know then in your heart that, as a man disciplines his son, the LORD your God disciplines you.
>
> —DEUTERONOMY 8:1–5

Purpose and Plans

Israel's wilderness season was a time of testing. It was a time of discipline. It was a time of humbling. Your wilderness season may be all those things too. But the wilderness season also has another purpose: "that he might make you *know* that man does not live by bread alone, but *man lives by every word that comes from the mouth of the* LORD" (v. 3, emphasis added). Don't miss that. I believe every wilderness season helps us learn that lesson. We will dig more into this in a later chapter.

Here's the other thing about wilderness seasons: When we are in them, we have a choice about how we handle it. If we respond in humility and learn whatever it is that God is trying to teach us, the wilderness season will end sooner. But if we choose to constantly complain, we're actually just extending our wilderness season.

There are no shortcuts in the wilderness. God has plans and purposes for you, and those plans will be fulfilled. If you try to take a shortcut and circumvent the Lord, it will actually be a longcut. If you don't believe me, ask the children of Israel—a journey that should have taken only a matter of days ended up taking them forty years.

When Jesus was in the wilderness, the devil came to tempt Him. (The devil does that to us too.) He started with Jesus' physical hunger, with His flesh. The devil said, "If you are the Son of God, command these stones to become loaves of bread" (Matt. 4:3). Jesus' response was to quote a familiar verse: "Man shall not live by bread alone, but by every word that comes from the mouth of God" (v. 4). Jesus used the lesson the Israelites learned in the wilderness to defeat the devil during His own time in the wilderness. Score one for Jesus.

The devil's next challenge to Jesus was to prove God's

care. The devil was appealing to the pride of life. He told Jesus to throw Himself from the pinnacle of the temple, and he even quoted Scripture. (The devil knows the Word of God. That's why it's so important that you know it too. You don't want to fall for it when the devil twists the Word into something God never intended.) Jesus responded with another Scripture quote: "You shall not put the Lord your God to the test" (v. 7). Score another one for Jesus.

Then Satan took Jesus "to a very high mountain and showed him all the kingdoms of the world and their glory" (v. 8). The devil knows how the desires of the eyes work, so he offered to give Jesus everything He saw. The devil offered Jesus power and influence if He would bow down and worship him. But the devil was actually offering Jesus something He already had.

Again, the devil does that with us too. We have abundant life, freedom, peace, hope, love, joy, grace, mercy, forgiveness, redemption, and every spiritual blessing in Christ, but the devil tries to make us think we are missing out. He is constantly trying to convince us that what we have in Christ is not enough. The devil is a liar. Jesus is enough—He is more than enough.

So when the devil tempted Jesus the third time, Jesus again fought back with the sword of the Spirit—also known as the Word of God—and said, "You shall worship the Lord your God and him only shall you serve" (v. 10). Final score: Jesus, three; Satan, zero.

The tests in the wilderness season allow us to see the power of God. They allow us to see the supernatural. That is why we must walk by faith, not by sight, especially in the wilderness seasons. And that is why humility is so important. We don't want to miss out on the supernatural because

Purpose and Plans

we are blinded by pride or because we are viewing the tests through our natural eyes rather than the eyes of faith.

Jesus was led into the wilderness by the Holy Spirit. That's very significant because we often think the devil is behind our trials and our suffering. We don't like to think that God will lead us into the wilderness. But He does. When the Holy Spirit led Jesus into the wilderness, it demonstrated that the testing was not outside God's will but was part of His plan. Hebrews 4:15 says, "For we do not have a high priest who is unable to sympathize with our weaknesses, but one who in every respect has been tempted as we are, yet without sin." And 1 John 2:16 says, "For all that is in the world—the desires of the flesh and the desires of the eyes and pride of life—is not from the Father but is from the world." Jesus dealt with all the kinds of temptations we face in this world, and because of that, He can sympathize with us in our weaknesses. That was just a small part of God's plan.

Jesus' time in the wilderness also shows us Jesus wasn't abandoned. He was empowered and guided by the Spirit, even in the midst of His trial. So the Holy Spirit doesn't abandon us either. He is with us, even in the moments of spiritual wilderness.

What we call suffering actually gives glory to God. It also brings new life to us. We say no to the flesh and yes to the Spirit. We deny ourselves and become conformed to the image of Christ. Our faith is strengthened, and we have victory in Jesus. We experience the supernatural.

If you are in a wilderness season, don't lose heart. God has a purpose for it. He has a plan. He is working all things together for your good. Don't forget what happens after a wilderness season. The children of Israel entered the Promised Land. The angels came and ministered to Jesus, and then He started His earthly ministry. Elijah got to hear the still, small voice of God, and then God took care of his enemies. I could go on, but you get the point. While the supernatural occurs during the wilderness season, it is also a time of preparation for the supernatural. Don't miss out on it.

Little Things

God will hide things in the things we think are insignificant. God will do the supernatural through the little things of life.

When I got out of prison, I thought I would be an evangelist. Never in a million years did I think I would be pastoring or doing anything I'm doing right now. I just thought I would spread the gospel everywhere through evangelism. Then one day, this guy asked me to help him with Spanish translation at a service for his church. I went and helped him out. It was a little thing. But then he said, "Hey, why don't you come here and be my Spanish pastor?"

My wife and I initially thought, "No way." But we fasted and prayed, and the Lord told us yes. During that time, God gave me the heart of a pastor, and my whole life changed.

Going to translate that day was such a small thing, but it was a step toward fulfilling the purpose God has for me. It wasn't what I expected at all, and I never would have expected God to change my heart in such a supernatural way through something so insignificant. But that is how He works. It may seem crazy, but it isn't. It's God.

Think about how God hid the provision to feed a crowd of five thousand men, plus women and children. Jesus,

Purpose and Plans

His disciples, and the crowd following them were up on a mountain. There was no Chick-fil-A to be found. And even if they could find a Chick-fil-A or another restaurant, how could they afford to feed a crowd that likely numbered at least fifteen thousand? But God does the supernatural through the little things. He hid the provision with a little boy. He took the contents of a little boy's lunch box—five loaves and two fish—and worked a miracle of multiplication. (See John 6:1–14 and Matthew 14:21.)

Sometimes we overlook the little things. We think, "How could God work through a child?" But God's Word tells us that an eight-year-old king named Josiah repaired the temple, destroyed the high places of idols, and "made a covenant before the Lord, to walk after the Lord and to keep his commandments and his testimonies and his statutes with all his heart and all his soul, to perform the words of this covenant that were written in this book. And all the people joined in the covenant" (2 Kings 23:3). Jesus said that God has hidden things "from the wise and understanding and revealed them to little children" (Matt. 11:25). Jesus also said, "Whoever receives one such child in my name receives me, and whoever receives me, receives not me but him who sent me" (Mark 9:37).

We also may think, "There were thousands of people to feed. Why even bother with a few loaves and fish?" But miracles of multiplication are never too hard for God. What seems insufficient in our hands can become more than enough when blessed by God. A widow was in so much debt that her children were going to be taken as slaves. All she had was one jar of oil, but God multiplied that oil so much that the widow could pay all her debts and still have plenty of money for her family to live on.

(See 2 Kings 4:1–7.) Psalm 40:5 says, "You have multiplied, O LORD my God, your wondrous deeds and your thoughts toward us; none can compare with you! I will proclaim and tell of them, yet they are more than can be told."

We don't have a problem with the big things, but nobody tends to look at the little things. However, Jesus is into the little things. Faithfulness involves being diligent and dependable in our service to God and His kingdom. It means using our talents and resources faithfully, even in the little things.

In Matthew 25:14–30 Jesus told the story of a master who entrusted his servants with different amounts of money before leaving on a journey. Upon his return he praised the servants who invested the money wisely and increased it, calling each of them a "good and faithful servant" (vv. 21, 23). But the servant who buried his talent out of fear was reprimanded. The parable illustrates the importance of being diligent and faithful with the responsibilities and opportunities God gives us, no matter how big or small.

The Lord has things in places that may seem insignificant to us, but they're totally important to Him. And that's the way He works. As humans we pretty much just like big things. We like shiny things. We like flashy things. So it's easy to overlook the supernatural when it involves the small things. However, when we do the little things well, Jesus will have us do the big things too.

When Ruthy and I were getting ready to start our church, I was praying and heard the Lord tell me to wake up at 5:00 a.m. and go teach at a homeless shelter. It was a little thing. There weren't going to be people considered important by the world there. There wasn't going to be an offering. There wasn't going to be an honorarium, a payment for my preaching. There weren't going to be TV cameras or podcasters broadcasting live. I was just going to teach a group of homeless people.

I obeyed, being faithful with a little thing. I got up at 5:00 a.m., went to the homeless shelter, and taught a message on time. After I was done, a guy came up to me. He looked like all the homeless people at the shelter. He said, "I want to do something for you. How can I help?"

I was thinking, "How can a homeless guy help me?" I didn't really know what to say, so I told him he could get me a cup of coffee.

He said, "No, no. How can I help you?"

I had a table where I was giving away free books, so I asked, "Do you want to help me at the table with the free stuff?"

He said, "You're not understanding." He introduced himself and told me he was the one who started the homeless shelter years earlier. "Your message really spoke to my heart. I'm not here all the time, but this is God's appointed time, so here I am. I want to help with your ministry. Can I help you start your nonprofit? Can I help you pay for it?"

I was tripping out. Here was this guy I thought was homeless, and he was offering to help me get the nonprofit started. I thought, "This is crazy!" But it wasn't crazy. It was God.

The guy took me to lunch, and he gave me a $15,000 check to help get the church started.

Jesus told a story to His disciples:

> When the Son of Man comes in his glory, and all the angels with him, then he will sit on his glorious throne. Before him will be gathered all the nations, and he will separate people one from another as a

> shepherd separates the sheep from the goats. And he will place the sheep on his right, but the goats on the left. Then the King will say to those on his right, "Come, you who are blessed by my Father, inherit the kingdom prepared for you from the foundation of the world. For I was hungry and you gave me food, I was thirsty and you gave me drink, I was a stranger and you welcomed me, I was naked and you clothed me, I was sick and you visited me, I was in prison and you came to me." Then the righteous will answer him, saying, "Lord, when did we see you hungry and feed you, or thirsty and give you drink? And when did we see you a stranger and welcome you, or naked and clothe you? And when did we see you sick or in prison and visit you?" And the King will answer them, "Truly, I say to you, as you did it to one of the least of these my brothers, you did it to me."
>
> —MATTHEW 25:31–40

Don't miss your blessing because it's packaged in a different way than what you think it should look like. Don't miss out on the supernatural just because it isn't what you expected. Don't miss your miracle because your pride won't allow you to do the little things. God ministers to us in ways that we cannot always comprehend, but it's through these tests that God reveals His power.

During the times of testing, allow the Word to sustain you. Accept the Word, write it on your heart, believe it way down in the depths of your being. People say, "All you gotta do is speak to it." But if you're saying something with your mouth that you actually don't believe in your heart, you may be walking in the opposite direction of what your mouth is saying.

It's in the little things and the lonely places that we prove ourselves capable of big things. If you want to be a person who sees God moving supernaturally in the big things, cultivate a habit of doing little things well. Take your gift and fan the flames.

ADVANCE THE KINGDOM

The purpose of the supernatural also includes advancing the kingdom of God. It's all about taking territory, right? Everything is about enlarging God's kingdom. It's about building His kingdom. Everything we do is about the kingdom "on earth as it is heaven" (Matt. 6:10). You will miss the supernatural if you are working to advance yourself rather than the kingdom of God. You can't say, "Your will be done," if you're still holding on to your own will.

That's why I'm always telling people that when advancing the kingdom of God, you need to take the territory inside you first. Everything supernatural that happens on the outside starts with the supernatural that's happening in your heart.

Think about when Noah built the ark. It definitely seemed crazy, but it was definitely a God thing. And the ark was built for other people to get on. It wasn't just about Noah. He built the ark, and others were saved because of it.

We mess up when we stop building the kingdom. If you build something just for you, you miss the kingdom. I've especially seen this happen with people whose lives are in shambles when they get saved. God does supernatural work in their lives, and they start doing very well—and then they forget the kingdom. They start building for themselves.

Building the kingdom is never about an event. It's about our hearts. The more we get our hearts right, the more we start building the kingdom.

It's like squeezing a donut. I used to live about a block away from Cake Boss in Hoboken, New Jersey. My mom would always bring donuts home from Cake Boss. I used to open the box and squeeze all the filled donuts to see what was in them. I would get in trouble for it, but I didn't want to take a big bite and find out I had a lemon-filled donut. Yuck! I wanted Bavarian cream. But thinking about that always reminds me that you don't know what's inside something until it gets squeezed. So what comes out of you when you get squeezed? What's in your heart?

Jesus said, "The kingdom of God is within you" (Luke 17:21, NKJV). When you are building the kingdom of God in yourself and you get squeezed, there's a difference. People notice that difference, and that builds the kingdom on the outside.

Everybody in the world knows what it looks like when someone gets squeezed and has a meltdown or an explosion. If that is what you look like when you get squeezed, you still have territory to take for the kingdom inside you. Sometimes we give ourselves the room to *not* tap into the supernatural. We justify it, saying it's OK to be who we are because we are still growing, God is still working on us, God knows our hearts, and no one is perfect. And all those things are true. I get the process. But if you continue to use all that as an excuse, you'll end up doing it the rest of your life. If you're constantly trying to modify your behavior, you may be modifying the rest of your life because you in your own power can't fix yourself and set

Purpose and Plans

yourself free. That's why it's about the kingdom. Every kingdom has a king, and the king says what happens.

This is why it's important for Jesus to be Lord of your life, to be the King of your heart. If He's just Jesus from down the street, you don't have to listen to Him. You don't have to submit to His will and His Word.

If you want to see the supernatural in your life, if you want to see God doing great things in you and through you, you need to submit your heart issues to the Holy Spirit. You need to lean on Him when you get squeezed. You need to continually submit your issues to the Word of God. The more you do that, the more that people will see the kingdom of God in you when you're squeezed. It will happen naturally because you'll have been filling yourself with Jesus. And the kingdom of God will advance.

It's all part of God's purposes and plans.

Chapter 3
CRAZY CHARACTERS

THE BIBLE IS full of crazy stories. It's full of examples of men and women of God who were called to do something crazy in order for God's plans and purposes to be fulfilled on the earth. These crazy characters demonstrate that God can use anyone and that He is not bound by human logic. Their stories of crazy faith inspire us to step out in crazy faith too—for when we do, we will experience the supernatural.

NOAH: OBEDIENCE IN THE FACE OF THE IMPOSSIBLE

Let's start with the story of Noah. Imagine being told by God to build an ark because a flood is coming. Now imagine that you don't know what a flood is because there has never been one before—in fact, you've never even seen rain before because the earth has been watered by a mist coming up from the ground (Gen. 2:6). Imagine telling your wife, "Honey, I've found favor with the Lord, so I have to build a 450-foot boat in the backyard! There might be a bit of a zoo in the backyard too." Noah's wife must have thought he was out of his mind. I'm sure his friends and neighbors thought the same thing.

But Noah trusted God and followed His command. The Lord gave Noah specific instructions about everything—the dimensions of the ark, the materials to use, the number of decks, and whom and what to bring with him into the ark. "And Noah did this. He did everything that God had commanded him" (Gen. 6:22, CSB). Even with the help of his three sons it had to have taken a long time to build the ark using hand tools. I imagine Noah was continually being criticized for obeying God, because no one believed a flood could actually happen—after all, it had never happened before. I'm sure "Noah, that's crazy!" was a constant refrain. But when the rains came and the waters rose, no one thought Noah was crazy anymore. What had seemed crazy turned out to be the very plan of salvation for Noah and his family.

Noah is an example of trusting God's word, even when the fulfillment takes a long time. The first few weeks after God spoke to Noah were probably exciting. Everyone was talking about it, and Noah was probably riding high on the fact that he had found favor with the Lord and been chosen for this task. But then weeks turned to years, and he was still building. He was still waiting for the rain to come. But Noah believed what God had spoken to him, so much so that nothing else mattered.

Noah had a little faith in a big God, and that was enough to sustain him when times were disheartening. He was operating in the power of God. He was building based on what God said. And even though it took a really long time, he remained faithful and continued to believe God.

Sometimes God calls us to do things that others don't

understand—and even we may not understand it. God's instructions may not always make sense to us, but His plans are perfect. Our role is to trust and obey, even when others think it's nuts. What appears crazy, when done in faith and obedience, may be the act that leads to our deliverance.

Abraham: Faith Beyond Reason

Abraham was called to leave his homeland and go to a place he had never seen. The Lord told him,

> Go from your land, your relatives, and your father's house to the land that I will show you. I will make you into a great nation, I will bless you, I will make your name great, and you will be a blessing. I will bless those who bless you, I will curse anyone who treats you with contempt, and all the peoples on earth will be blessed through you.
> —Genesis 12:1–3, csb

I don't know which was crazier—Noah telling his wife about the gigantic boat and the zoo in the backyard or Abraham telling his wife they were moving.

"Start packing up, Sarah. We're moving."

"Where are we going?"

"I don't know."

"What do you mean you don't know? Why are we moving if you don't know where we are going?"

"The Lord told me to leave this land. Once we leave, He will show us where to go."

"That's crazy!"

Even though everyone thought he was crazy, Abraham left his homeland, "as the Lord had told him"

(Gen. 12:4, CSB). But God wasn't finished with Abraham. The Lord made a covenant with him, promising him that his descendants would be as numerous as the stars, even though he and his wife Sarah were old and childless. It would have been easy for Abraham to dismiss God's promise as unrealistic. "That's crazy!" someone might have said. But Abraham didn't say, "That's crazy." He "believed the LORD, and [God] credited it to him as righteousness" (Gen. 15:6, CSB). Eventually, Isaac was born, and through him the promise the Lord made to Abraham was fulfilled.

Faith sometimes requires us to step into the unknown, trusting that God's promises, no matter how improbable, are true. Faith requires us to step out of our comfort zones, trusting that God's Word will come to pass, even when the path ahead is unclear. That's difficult for us. We want to be in the know. We want to know the plan. We want to know what every step is. Psalm 119:105 says, "Your word is a lamp for my feet" (CSB). God will provide the directions one step at a time, like a flashlight lights up your next step when you are walking through the darkness. When we don't want to move because we can't see as far ahead as we would like, we are walking by sight rather than by faith. Faith starts moving even when there is only enough light for the next step.

Joshua: Victory Through Obedience, Not Strategy

After Moses died, Joshua became the leader of the children of Israel. It was a big job because they were finally going to enter the Promised Land. And when the children

Crazy Characters

of Israel entered the land, they had to take possession of it. They had to conquer it. The first city they had to take was Jericho, a fortified, walled city that was closed up tight as the Israelites approached.

The Lord told Joshua,

> Look, I have handed Jericho, its king, and its best soldiers over to you. March around the city with all the men of war, circling the city one time. Do this for six days. Have seven priests carry seven ram's-horn trumpets in front of the ark. But on the seventh day, march around the city seven times, while the priests blow the rams' horns. When there is a prolonged blast of the horn and you hear its sound, have all the troops give a mighty shout. Then the city wall will collapse, and the troops will advance, each man straight ahead.
>
> —Joshua 6:2–5, csb

The plan God gave Joshua to conquer Jericho made no military sense. Marching around a fortified city in silence for six days and then shouting on the seventh day doesn't sound like a winning strategy. Yet Joshua and the Israelites obeyed, and on the seventh day, the walls of Jericho collapsed, just like God said they would. What seemed like a ridiculous plan was actually God's way of demonstrating His power.

God's methods don't always follow conventional wisdom. Sometimes His path to victory looks nothing like what we expect. Our role is to trust and obey, even when the plan seems strange. Joshua was willing to obey the Lord because his faith was strong. He had seen all the signs and wonders God had done in delivering Israel from slavery in Egypt and then in leading them through the wilderness for forty years. But that wasn't the only reason his faith was strong. Exodus 33:11 says, "The LORD would speak with Moses face to face, just as a man speaks with his friend, then Moses would return to the camp. His assistant, the young man Joshua son of Nun, would not leave the inside of the tent" (CSB). Did you catch that? Even after Moses left the tent—referring to the tabernacle, or the Tent of Meeting, the place where the presence of God was—Joshua stayed put. He stayed in the presence of God. He was taking territory for the kingdom of God inside his heart long before he started taking territory in the Promised Land.

It is easy to be tempted to fight our own way, to rely on our own strength. But when our faith is strong, when we have taken territory for the kingdom inside our own hearts by spending time in God's presence, we trust God to fight for us. And when we let the Lord fight for us, when we rely on His plan, the supernatural occurs: "For the LORD your God is the one who goes with you to fight for you against your enemies to give you victory" (Deut. 20:4, CSB).

GIDEON: THE WEAK MADE STRONG

Gideon was hiding when the Lord first appeared to him. He was threshing wheat in a winepress to hide it from the Midianites. Gideon wasn't brave. He chose to hide rather than face a fight, but when the Lord appeared to him through an angel, He called Gideon a "valiant warrior" (Judg. 6:12, CSB). The Lord told Gideon, "Go in the strength you have and deliver Israel from the grasp of Midian. I am sending you!" (Judg. 6:14, CSB). Gideon flipped out. He asked how he could possibly deliver Israel when he was the youngest in the weakest family of his tribe. In other words, Gideon thought it was crazy that God was sending him. Yet that is exactly what God did.

Gideon did not feel equipped for what God had called him to do, and he asked God to confirm his mission over and over again. And God confirmed it. The Lord had chosen Gideon, not for his own strength, not for his bravery, not for his wisdom, not for his leadership skills, but for his willingness to obey the word of the Lord.

God sent Gideon out to face the Midianite army, numbering around 135,000. Gideon had only 32,000 men in his army. But God said Gideon had too many. So Gideon told anyone who was afraid to turn back. His army then numbered 22,000. The Lord said that was still too many. Gideon ended up facing the Midianites with a whopping total of 300 men.

In human terms, 300 against 135,000 isn't just crazy—it's suicidal. How could Gideon ever hope to be victorious? But God's ways are not our ways, and nothing is too hard for Him. With God's help Gideon and his tiny army defeated the massive Midianite army. (See Judges 6–8.)

It has been said that God doesn't call the equipped; He equips the called. When God calls you to something for the kingdom, it doesn't matter if it seems crazy. It doesn't matter if it seems like it is something that is not in your power to do. It doesn't matter if you think you don't have the necessary skills for the assignment. When God calls you, He will give you what you need. His grace is sufficient for you, and His strength is made perfect in weakness (2 Cor. 12:9). And don't forget, "Not by might, nor by power, but by my Spirit, says the LORD of hosts" (Zech. 4:6).

When Gideon faced battle with the Midianites, it

looked like defeat was certain. But when defeat is certain in human terms, no one but God can get the glory when victory comes. God often reduces our resources to show us that the victory comes from Him. When we feel inadequate, that's when God can work powerfully through us. That's when we know the truth of Philippians 4:13: "I can do all things through Christ who strengthens me" (NKJV).

JEHOSHAPHAT: THE BATTLE IS THE LORD'S

In 2 Chronicles 20 King Jehoshaphat faced a coalition of three powerful armies. Instead of preparing for battle in the traditional way, Jehoshaphat "resolved to seek the LORD" (v. 3, CSB). But that wasn't enough for Jehoshaphat. He "proclaimed a fast for all Judah, who gathered to seek the LORD" (vv. 3–4, CSB).

The king stood in front of his people and prayed,

> LORD, God of our ancestors, are you not the God who is in heaven, and do you not rule over all the kingdoms of the nations? Power and might are in your hand, and no one can stand against you. Are you not our God who drove out the inhabitants of this land before your people Israel and who gave it forever to the descendants of Abraham your friend? They have lived in the land and have built you a sanctuary in it for your name and have said, "If disaster comes on us—sword or judgment, pestilence or famine—we will stand before this temple and before you, for your name is in this temple. We will cry out to you because of our distress, and you will hear and deliver."...
> We do not know what to do, but we look to you.
> —2 CHRONICLES 20:6–9, 12, CSB

Jehoshaphat sought the Lord, and the Lord answered. God said,

> Do not be afraid or discouraged because of this vast number, for the battle is not yours, but God's....You do not have to fight this battle. Position yourselves, stand still, and see the salvation of the LORD. He is with you, Judah and Jerusalem. Do not be afraid or discouraged. Tomorrow, go out to face them, for the LORD is with you.
> —2 CHRONICLES 20:15, 17, CSB

God instructed him to send out worshippers in front of the army. As they praised the Lord, singing, "Give thanks to the LORD, for his faithful love endures forever" (v. 21, CSB), God set ambushes against their enemies. Their enemies ended up turning against each other, and they annihilated themselves. King Jehoshaphat and his army didn't have to fight at all. All they had to do was worship. What seemed like a crazy battle plan resulted in a miraculous victory.

Sometimes we face battles that seem unwinnable. It seems like we are being attacked on all sides. But don't be afraid or discouraged. Battles aren't always won with swords and shields. Sometimes battles are won with praise and worship. When we place our focus on God instead of the problem, He fights for us. Sometimes we just need to position ourselves, stand still, and see the salvation of the Lord.

PETER: FAITH DEFYING NATURE

Immediately after Jesus fed the five thousand, He made the disciples get into the boat and cross over to the other side of the Sea of Galilee while He went up the mountain to pray. The disciples were in the boat all night, struggling against the wind and being battered by the waves. Then the disciples saw someone walking on the water, and they flipped out, thinking it was a ghost.

> Jesus spoke to them. "Have courage! It is I. Don't be afraid."
> "Lord, if it's you," Peter answered him, "command me to come to you on the water."
> He said, "Come."
> And climbing out of the boat, Peter started walking on the water and came toward Jesus. But when he saw the strength of the wind, he was afraid, and beginning to sink he cried out, "Lord, save me!"
> Immediately Jesus reached out his hand, caught hold of him, and said to him, "You of little faith, why did you doubt?"
> —MATTHEW 14:27–31, CSB

When Jesus called Peter to step out of the boat and walk on water, it was an invitation to do the impossible. It was an invitation to experience the supernatural. What seemed like a reckless decision—getting out of a boat in the middle of all the wind and waves—was actually an opportunity for Peter to experience the supernatural power of God.

As long as Peter kept his eyes on Jesus, he stayed above the waves. But when he focused on the storm around him, he began to sink. It's like that sometimes when we step out in faith. When Jesus calls us to climb out of the boat, we do it in faith. Then the supernatural occurs. But sometimes we let the supernatural flip us out, and we take our eyes off Jesus. When we take our eyes off Jesus, we lose that connection with the supernatural, and we start to sink. That's why we need to remember the importance of "fixing our eyes on Jesus, the author and perfecter of faith" (Heb. 12:2, NASB).

Faith requires stepping out of the boat, even when the waves look threatening. When God calls us to take risks, it's not reckless—it's an opportunity to walk on water.

Jesus: The Resurrection

Finally, let's consider the resurrection of Jesus Christ. When some women arrived at the garden tomb that Sunday morning, an angel told them, "He is not here. For he has risen, just as he said" (Matt. 28:6, CSB). The grave could not hold the King of kings!

To many the idea of a man rising from the dead after three days is beyond belief. It's the ultimate "That's crazy!"

But the resurrection is the cornerstone of our faith. Without it our hope is in vain. The apostle Paul wrote, "If Christ has not been raised, then our proclamation is in vain, and so is your faith" (1 Cor. 15:14, CSB). If Jesus had stayed dead, it would have meant He was a man just like everyone else, rather than the Son of God.

But He is the Son of God. He is the Messiah, the Anointed One. He is the Lamb of God, slain before the foundation of the world, who takes away the sins of the world. He is the living Word. He is "the Alpha and the Omega, the Beginning and the End, the First and the Last" (Rev. 22:13, MEV).

Through the resurrection, God demonstrated His power over death. He demonstrated His ability to restore life. He demonstrated that nothing is impossible with God. The resurrection shows us God can bring life out of death, hope out of despair, and victory out of defeat. What the world sees as impossible God makes possible. That means there is nothing in your life that God can't handle. Nothing is too hard for Him.

Throughout Scripture, God continuously worked in ways that defied human logic. He proved over and over that He is the God of all the earth. He fights for us. He loves us. He calls us His own. And "with God all things are possible" (Matt. 19:26). What appears as a setback, an impossibility, or even a failure is often a setup for God's glory to be revealed. His ways are higher, His plans are greater, and His power is limitless.

So when life seems chaotic or when God's direction feels confusing, remember—what seems crazy to us is just God doing what only He can do. He is in the business of turning the impossible into reality.

Chapter 4
IMPOSSIBLE? OR IMMEASURABLY MORE THAN YOU CAN IMAGINE?

THERE ARE SOME people who think that God no longer performs miracles the way He did for the people in the Bible. They think the signs and wonders have ceased. But God is still in the business of the supernatural. He is still "able to do immeasurably more than all we ask or imagine, according to his power that is at work within us" (Eph. 3:20, NIV).

The Bible says that we overcome the devil by the blood of the Lamb and the word of our testimony (Rev. 12:11). When we share testimonies of the supernatural at work in our lives, it builds faith—both in us and in others. It defeats the devil's lie that God doesn't do miracles anymore. When we tell stories that make people say, "That's crazy," we can then tell them, "No, that's God!" They aren't crazy stories; they're God stories. Here are some to build your faith.

A DIVINE SETUP

I have a son named Jonathan. When I went to prison the last time, I hadn't seen him in eighteen or nineteen years. One day, about four years after I got saved, I was sitting on my bunk in prison when a nineteen-year-old kid walked in. I said, "Hey. What's up? What's your name?"

He said his name was Johnathan.

I was on fire with the Holy Ghost, and I thought that even though I had missed out on being a father to my Jonathan, I could be a father to this Johnathan. I wound up discipling Johnathan as we were in prison together.

On the flip side was Johnathan's mom. Before I even met her, Johnathan and I were praying for her. We had a prayer circle that met by a tree at noon, and Johnathan wanted to pray for his mom to get a Bible and to find a church. We would pray for his mom to get closer to Jesus. I was getting reports back from Johnathan on how God was working in his mom's life, and his mom and I eventually started writing letters to each other.

Meanwhile, Johnathan's aunts were telling his mom, "You need a man."

She responded, "I'm not going to go searching for him. God is going to bring him to me."

Johnathan's aunts would then laugh and say, "What do you think? God is going to send him through the mail?"

And it turns out that God did send him through the mail, because Johnathan's mom—the woman whose son I discipled and fathered, the woman I prayed would get closer to Jesus, the woman who got letters from me while I was in prison—is Ruthy, who is now my wife.

That's God! It was a divine setup, which is the best kind.

We're still praying for Johnathan. He ended up going back to prison after he got out, but we are still believing for him. I also feel like the enemy has been beating up on Johnathan since he was the one who brought Ruthy and me together, and the enemy is not happy about all the things God is doing in us and through us to advance the kingdom of God. I don't think Johnathan really knows how to fight in the spirit realm, but we keep praying for him and discipling him. He is coming home soon, and I believe his testimony is going to be mighty.

Restoration

God has also been restoring my family. The Lord is the restorer, the repairer of the breach (Isa. 58:12), and He has demonstrated that in restoring my relationships with my kids. That's God!

When I got out of prison, I got in contact with my son Jonathan, trying to start restoring our relationship. His grandmother had been taking care of him, but he was having some trouble. So one day, his grandmother called and said, "I need you to be his dad now." So Jonathan came down and moved in with us.

We started walking with him and discipling him, and he went through his own process, his own faith journey. And the Lord changed him. It was amazing. But then my other two kids came to visit. There was such a change in Jonathan that his older brother wanted to beat him up because he thought Jonathan was lying and just putting on a show. He told Jonathan to tell the truth about who he really was. He didn't believe anyone could change like that—but people can change like that because that is exactly what God does.

I told my other two kids that they had "tasted a bit of heaven." I used those exact words. They tasted some of heaven because they were in our house; they tasted love, they tasted joy, and they tasted peace. They were able to "taste and see that the LORD is good" (Ps. 34:8). I told them that when they left, they were not going to get that anymore—and so they would come back. That's what happened. They both went home, and then they both called, saying, "We want to move there with you." So they both moved down here.

Now all my kids go to church, and our whole family is restored. We have six kids—including Jonathan and Johnathan—and a dog named Max. We're like the Hispanic Brady Bunch. My daughter works for the church, and my son Jonathan is one of the youth pastors. It's amazing. I got to baptize them both. I'm waiting to baptize the other ones. Jay, Valery, Josh, and Johnathan are all doing well and growing in the Lord.

God is turning "the hearts of fathers to their children and the hearts of children to their fathers" (Mal. 4:6). In this generation, when fatherlessness is at epidemic levels, you may think, "That's crazy!" But that's God!

Give It All

When Ruthy and I got married, we didn't have much. We only had Walmart wedding rings. But I wanted to get Ruthy a house, and I had started saving money for it. I had saved up about $7,000, which was the most I had ever saved in my entire life.

I was praying one day, and the Lord told me to give Him the money.

I said, "Lord, this is all I have saved. How am I gonna get the house?"

He said, "Give it to Me."

I did not want to give the Lord all that money, so I tried

Impossible? Or Immeasurably More Than You Can Imagine?

to get Ruthy to go against it. I asked her, "What would you do if the Lord told you to give Him all our savings?"

She said, "I would just give it."

That was not the answer I wanted. I kept turning it over in my mind, thinking maybe Ruthy answered that way because she didn't know how much money it was or didn't realize it was my life savings. But I just said, "OK."

So I went to church, and I was crying. Just in case you missed it, I really didn't want to give God all that money. It felt like a million dollars to me. A friend came over and asked what was going on, and I told him, "God told me to give Him everything."

I wanted to hold on to that money. I even tried to convince God to let me make payments instead of giving it to Him all at once. But God's instructions were clear: Give it all. So I did. I got an envelope, and I put it all in.

About two weeks later, a guy who had never been to my church came with his wife. He had just sold his company. He had been watching John Hagee on television, and—this is wild—he heard him say, "Go to Get Wrapped Church and tithe." So he came to church, and he handed me two checks. He said, "This one is for the church, and this one is for you and your wife."

I've had people give me checks personally before, and I thought it was maybe $500 or something similar. I opened the check for me and Ruthy, and it wasn't $500. It was $50,000!

That money moved us into our house, and I was able to give my wife a new wedding ring.

The other check, the one for the church, helped Get Wrapped get moving and growing.

God did everything I had been praying about, and the

way He did it was wild. It was completely unexpected. But it was God.

Hair and Healing

There was a lady named Maria at our church who was battling breast cancer, and we were praying and believing for her healing. Maria shared with my wife that she would soon reach the point in her treatment when she would have to shave her head. Ruthy reminded Maria that beauty is on the inside and offered to go with Maria when she shaved her head.

Then one day, Maria called Ruthy and told her she had just shaved her head. She did it on her own because she felt like she just had to get it over with. Maria was understandably upset, and she told Ruthy that she was going to be so embarrassed at church on Sunday, showing up with a shaved head. Ruthy reminded Maria again that beauty is on the inside. She reminded her that everyone at the church loved her and that it would be OK.

When Ruthy got off the phone, she started praying for Maria. The Holy Spirit prompted Ruthy to shave her head too, and Ruthy had complete peace about it. She told me what she was going to do. I asked her if she was sure, and she told me again that she had complete peace about shaving her head. My wife has beautiful hair, and she loves her hair. And while there are times when someone might shave their head as a kind gesture to a cancer patient, this was more than that. God put this act into Ruthy's heart. She was following the Holy Spirit's lead.

Ruthy decided to do it after the service on Sunday, and I asked Pastor Vinnie, who is a barber, to bring his

Impossible? Or Immeasurably More Than You Can Imagine?

clipper to church. But on Sunday morning as I started telling the story during the service, it seemed right for Ruthy to shave her head then rather than waiting until after the service. And as Ruthy's beautiful, long hair fell to the ground, another woman in leadership at the church decided to shave her head too. Then another one. Then some of the guys, including me, got in on the action. In all, about twelve people, half of whom were women, shaved their heads that morning. For all of us it was an act of faith, as we believed that God was going to heal Maria.

We had a first-time visitor that morning. He and his wife had been looking for a church. He vividly remembers that day:

> We had already been to ten churches and just couldn't find the right one. But we knew...[God] would let us both know when we found it.
>
> And...when we walked in Get Wrapped, it was when Maria was having cancer, and her hair was all falling out....Pastor Vinnie was up there, and they were shaving everybody's hair in support of her. And what really got me...[is] for a guy to do that...it hurts, but when the women started getting up there...
>
> ...Pastor Ruthy had this long, flowing, black hair, curly—it was beautiful, beautiful hair. And I watched how loving she was and how giving she was to go up there and lead the women....[It] was probably eighteen, twenty inches long...just falling to the ground, and before you knew it, she had no hair left....That totally moved me.
>
> ...When we got to the parking lot, Michelle was like, "What do you think?"

And I said, "We found our home church. We found it."[1]

The man who visited that day is now our financial pastor, Pastor Gregg. He knew if people were that giving and had that kind of relationship with the Lord, this was the kind of place he wanted to be. And that's God.

That was twelve years ago, and Maria is still alive. She is cancer free. That is supernatural. And when Pastor Gregg shared the story not too long ago, it still created awe and wonder. That's God too.

We believe Maria was healed because of our obedience. When God speaks to us, we need to obey, even when it's hard. Every single choice we make is about being made in His image to give Him glory. The key is listening to the Holy Spirit rather than trying to duplicate what someone else did. God has specific directions for His children. He may tell someone to give an offering and tell someone else to fast and pray. Shaving your head is not going to be effective when the Spirit is telling you to fast and pray.

ALIVE FOR A REASON

When Vaughn was seven years old, he started having headaches. Doctors did not have any answers to give his mother, Pastor Megan at our church, and the rest of the family. Then one day, Vaughn collapsed. An MRI and a CAT scan revealed that Vaughn had a medulloblastoma, an aggressive brain tumor with a grim prognosis. The surgery to remove the tumor, even if it were successful, would likely permanently disable Vaughn physically and mentally, putting him in a wheelchair and giving him the intellectual ability of a four-year-old.

Impossible? Or Immeasurably More Than You Can Imagine?

The family called on the church to pray for Vaughn. The tumor was removed successfully, and Vaughn was doing well—until he developed a life-threatening infection. Megan was in a tailspin, questioning her faith. But when she finally realized she had no control and that only God could control the situation, she had a breakthrough. She surrendered control to the Lord. She surrendered her son to the Lord.

The church family gathered to pray for Vaughn once again. His fever broke the next day, and Vaughn made a full recovery from both the brain tumor and the infection. As I write, he is now in high school, and just the other day, he was telling me about how he wants to become an FBI agent—the same kid who was supposed to be in a wheelchair with the mind of a preschooler.

Vaughn said, "I had God by my side and a lot of people praying for me. He kept me alive for a reason. I would feel like it's crazy that it happened to me, but like something our church likes to say...that's not crazy, that's God."[2]

STOLEN TRAILER RESTORED

At the church we have a trailer where we keep all our stuff that we use for outreach and some other ministry things. The contents of the trailer are worth a lot of money.

The trailer got stolen. Someone called me to tell me about it, and I just couldn't believe it. So of course, we were trying to find the trailer to see if we could get it back, but we were unsuccessful. Somebody else bought the trailer from the guy who stole it. When the man who purchased the trailer looked inside, he saw all the stuff with the Get Wrapped logo and realized he had purchased a stolen trailer. He looked us up online and called the church office. He told us, "Come pick it up. I ain't getting in the way of God."

We went and picked up the trailer. All our stuff was still in it. Nothing was missing. Even though the man had paid a lot of money to purchase the trailer, he gave it back to us without a second thought. That's God!

Crazy Generosity

I had this financial plan. It took me months to put it together. In 2017 I started investing personally in publicly traded companies. I started learning about stocks, but then I left it alone for a while. Then a couple of years ago I felt like the Lord impressed something on my heart. The best way I can explain it is it was a strong conviction. When people ask me how I invest, I don't know what to tell them other than that I pray, and if I feel like God gives me a conviction to do something, I do it.

I felt like the Lord was telling me to buy Bitcoin. Remember, I've never had a lot of savings or money for retirement because I sold drugs most of my life. I only had a small amount of money in savings, so I tried to borrow money to invest because the conviction in my heart was so strong. (Sidenote: If you don't know the Lord is telling you to do something, don't borrow money, because then it's reckless.) But I couldn't shake the conviction, which is why I tried to borrow. My wife thought I was going crazy. My financial pastor was laughing at me and saying, "I don't have it."

I couldn't borrow any money, so I started scraping together everything we had. Then God opened a door or two for me to make some money, and I took it all and did what God told me to do, which was get into Bitcoin. It was at $17,000, and then two years later it went up to $100,000, which gave me the initial capital to start investing in certain other things. I was working on my plan.

I talked to God and told Him I was going to pay my car off and then keep investing because I obviously was seeing some fruit. I wasn't trying to get rich; I was thinking about having some money for retirement, paying off my house, and things like that. So I'm talking to God about all this, and He asks, "Do you love Pastor Todd?" Pastor Todd is a part-time teaching pastor at Get Wrapped, and his wife, Tanya, works for us too.

"Yeah, Lord. I love Pastor Todd."

"What would you do for him?"

"Man, he's kind of struggling with the car stuff. Lord, when I get the money from this other investment, I will give him my car." My car was a BMW that was only one year old. I'd never given an offering like that in my life, but it came right out of my mouth.

The Lord challenged me, "So you're going to wait for Me to give you these finances?" Clear as day He said, "Juan, I want you to take the rest of the Bitcoin money, pay off the car, and give him the vehicle."

My plan already was to pay off the car, but it was so I wouldn't have a car payment, not so I could give away a practically brand-new car. I asked, "Give him the paid-off car? My brand-new car?"

"Yes, give him the vehicle. Juan, your worst-case scenario is you have another car payment. His worst-case scenario is he has no car and can't afford a car payment. So now it's your choice. Do you love Pastor Todd?"

It was so hard. I came up with every excuse for why not

to give it to him. I had this long list. But I heard the quiet, gentle voice of the Holy Spirit say, "It's your choice. If you love him, you give him the vehicle."

What's even crazier is that the Lord popped this on me a few days before we planned to teach on crazy generosity at church. And now God wanted me to demonstrate crazy generosity—even though it wasn't part of my plan.

I paid off the car and gave it to Pastor Todd.

Honestly, I cried that day. I felt like God had blessed me so much after I got out of prison, but it wasn't just for me. Giving Pastor Todd the car is the biggest offering I've ever given. It actually got me really, really nervous. I was hyperventilating a little bit, thinking, "I can't believe I'm doing this." But the reward of seeing Pastor Todd and his family super happy was amazing.

I texted Todd, "How's the car?"

He responded, "Incredible."

Don't hold on to things too tightly. When God is speaking to us, we need to just do it. And there's always a reward, whether physical or spiritual or both.

So now I have a car payment. That's OK because I can afford the car payment. And I have a few other investments I believe haven't come to full fruition yet, but I believe they will enable me to pay off my car. This story isn't finished yet.

You Can't Get a Passport!

Before I got saved, I was the guy who didn't pay child support. I was high on drugs, and even though my finances were such that I could pay child support, I didn't because I was rebellious.

So time passed, and I got saved. I got out of prison and

Impossible? Or Immeasurably More Than You Can Imagine?

got married, and I would always tell my wife that we would go to France one day. It was our dream trip. However, in the US you can't get a passport if you owe more than $2,500 in past-due child support. And let me tell you, I owed a whole lot more than $2,500. So whenever I mentioned the trip to France, my wife would laugh and tell me, "When are we going to go? You can't even leave the country. You can't get a passport because you don't have the money to pay all the child support you owe."

I would joke with her and tell her that when I went to France, I would go by myself and then take a picture and send it to her. "See? I'm in France!" We joked about it whenever we talked about it.

So during COVID, when everything was going bad and the economy was tanking, God blessed me with the money to pay off the past-due child support, which was almost $30,000. I actually flew out to Puerto Rico, went to the office over there, and paid the full amount.

And I was able to get a passport.

In a time when it seemed chaotic and dark, God was still faithful. I've since been to Israel and Africa. I'm going on a mission trip to Honduras this year. And my wife and I finally took our trip to France. We were actually able to spend three weeks in Europe. When we got the tickets, I teased my wife, "You don't need to pack. You're not going to France. You gotta stay here because you said I wouldn't ever be able to go." And we laughed, but it also built up my wife's faith.

God is the God of the impossible. And God wants to do things according to His will, so our hearts have to line up with His will. My desire to pay the past-due child support wasn't just about the child support. I wanted a clean slate. I wanted to be a man of integrity. The choices we make develop our character—for good or bad—and when we choose to pray and act according to the will of God, we shouldn't be surprised when the supernatural occurs.

Night Out with Jesus

Sometime after Ruthy and I got married, we started doing what we called Night Out with Jesus on our date nights. Instead of going to dinner and a movie ourselves, we would take our date night money and use it to bless someone else. For example, we would go into a restaurant and pay for someone else's meal. We would hang back and watch to see their faces when they found out their meal was paid for, and then we would run out of the restaurant all excited and go home.

I had this vision, this dream, to make Night Out with Jesus bigger, to have people doing it all over the planet. It started with our church. We started doing Night Out with Jesus several times throughout the year. We go to gas stations and grocery stores and pay for people's gas or groceries. Then we pray for them and help them encounter Jesus. We do things like buying five hundred pizzas for five dollars each to hand out and bless the community, with the goal of letting people know that Jesus loves them and wants to have an authentic relationship with them.

Sometimes people don't want to receive the blessing, but we tell them, "God is trying to get your attention. Don't look at what you're getting tangibly. Think about who is moving in the heart of the person trying to bless you, because He wants to talk to you." The results have been miraculous.

Impossible? Or Immeasurably More Than You Can Imagine?

The Lord can use anything, even a five-dollar pizza, to reach someone's heart. That's supernatural. That's God.

We had a Night Out with Jesus scheduled for March 28, 2025. Then a church in Ohio said they wanted to be involved in their hometown. Then a pastor in Dallas called to say he wanted his church to participate too. It was an amazing night full of supernatural, miraculous moments. One of my favorite moments happened at the end of that night. We always gather back at the church to share testimonies of how God moved. And then people come up to the altar to give whatever leftover money they have or anything else God puts on their hearts to give. It's a time of crazy generosity. Then we pray and ask God, "Who do we give the money to?"

Well, that night there was a man there who had just gotten out of prison after twenty-one years. He had watched me online when he was in prison, and when he got out, he decided to come to Get Wrapped. And we decided to give the money to him. That blessed my heart so much because I know what it's like when you first get out of prison. I know how hard it is.

But here's what's wild: At the same time that we were deciding to bless this man who'd just gotten out of prison, the church in Ohio was doing the same thing. The person they decided to give the money to had also just gotten out of prison. That's God!

As I write, the next Night Out with Jesus is scheduled for June 27. It's going to happen all over Texas in Houston, Galveston, Dallas, Fort Worth, Athens, and Abilene. It's also going to happen in Ohio, Colorado, Missouri, Illinois, and Washington. It started with just two people, but now look what God has done! We are seeing a miracle of multiplication, and that's God! It's like the loaves and fish in the feeding of the five thousand. Everybody has a piece of bread because they have the Bread of Life living in them. So they can take their bread, break it, and give it to someone else. And then they can break it and give it again. And again. And again. And the bread is never going to run out, no matter how many times we break it as we are reaching out to the lost and the hurting in our communities so they can encounter Jesus. God is so good!

Chapter 5
MOVE-A-MOUNTAIN FAITH

WHEN I LOOK at my life from the very beginning, it's like I started with a hole in the bottom of my shoe. I didn't have anything. And then God ordered my steps.

I always tell people that the first year of walking by faith is going to whoop you. It's not going to be easy because you'll want to keep going back to human logic. But human logic is what got you in trouble in the first place. When you go back to what you think is best, you end up falling for the enemy's lie that a life of bondage is better than a life of faith. You may be right on the edge of a supernatural move of God, but you look back at your old life and think, "It wasn't that bad"—just as the children of Israel did right before God parted the Red Sea so they could cross over on dry land.

You can't buy the devil's lies. Life in bondage is horrible. God has given you freedom; you need to stand fast. Galatians 5:1 says, "For freedom Christ has set us free; stand firm therefore, and do not submit again to a yoke of slavery." To stand firm in your freedom, you have to start walking out these thoughts that are super foreign. And they are super foreign because you are used to walking by sight rather than walking by faith. You have to train yourself to walk in faith. You have to train yourself to walk in the fear of the Lord, which is the beginning of wisdom.

Everything is about being made in His image. When you seek Him first, all the other stuff is going to be added to you: "But seek first the kingdom of God and his righteousness, and all these things will be provided for you" (Matt. 6:33, CSB).

I get that it's difficult when you first start walking by faith. I was very nervous when I started because I was already forty years old. I was looking at things like my finances and thinking, "Lord, I'm never going to pay off this house." But I started walking by faith. When the Lord told me to invest in Bitcoin, I invested in Bitcoin. When the Lord told me to give away my car, I gave away my car. And I have reaped a harvest by being obedient and walking by faith rather than by sight.

I'm the guy that got out of prison. Things like that shouldn't be happening to me, right? They should be happening to people who have been saved a lot longer than me, right? Wrong. God is interested in faith, not longevity. I didn't do those things with the thought of, "Ooh, I'm going to get rich." I did them because the Lord told me to, and "God gave the increase" (1 Cor. 3:6, MEV). As God gave the increase, He kept giving me directions, and I kept following them. I made the choice to walk by faith. I made the choice to obey God, and I saw supernatural results.

I've been doing these things by faith. God doesn't talk to me all the time like He did with the Bitcoin and the car, but since I'm constantly doing things to be made in His image, whenever He speaks to me, I think, "OK. God wants me to do this, so I'm going to do it. I'm going to mature. I'm going to do it out of love." When God asks you to do crazy things, you can only do them according to faith.

Faith is part of the fruit of the Spirit listed in Galatians 5:22–23. The Greek word for *faith* is *pistis*. It means faith or faith in God. It also means persuasion, the character of someone who can be relied upon, fidelity, belief, faithfulness, conviction, assurance, and reliance.[1]

Faith is divine persuasion by the One who can always be relied on. Divine persuasion means God speaks and the Holy Spirit moves you. You are operating by faith and moving in the direction the Spirit's wind blows.

When Faith Falters

Hebrews 11:1 says, "Now faith is the assurance of things hoped for, the conviction of things not seen." Faith in God is rooted in trust and belief in His promises and His character. Faith means you trust that God is who He says He is and that He will do what He says He will do.

Abraham is called the father of the faith. He trusted God's promises even when they seemed impossible. When the Lord made a covenant with Abraham, He changed his name from Abram to Abraham: "The word of the Lord came to Abram in a vision: 'Fear not, Abram, I am your shield; your reward shall be very great'" (Gen. 15:1). In other words, God was saying, "I will protect you, and your reward is going to be awesome." Remember that God had given Abraham a promise before; He said He was going to "make of [him] a great nation" (Gen. 12:2). Abraham already had that promise, but then we fast-forward to when the Lord appeared to Abraham again, and Abraham said, "O Lord God, what will you give me, for I continue childless, and the heir of my house is Eliezer of Damascus?... Behold, you have given me no offspring, and a member of my household will be my heir" (Gen. 15:2–3).

The father of faith had faith that was faltering. Abraham was basically saying, "I don't know if I believe this anymore." Have you ever gotten to a difficult spot in your walk of faith? Have you ever been impatient to see the promises of God fulfilled in your life? Has your faith ever been shaken? That's where Abraham was. But the beauty of it is that when his faith was faltering, the word of God came to him.

When your faith is faltering, you need the Word of the Lord. You need the Word to encourage you. You need the Word to remind you of the truth. You need the Word to remind you that God is faithful. You need the Word to remind you that God always keeps His promises. You actually have an advantage over Abraham in this area. You have easy access to the Word of the Lord. It's on the shelf or the bedside table in your house. It's on your phone. It's on your computer and your tablet. You can read it. You can listen to it. Abraham didn't have any of those options, so the Lord appeared to him in a vision, and God may do that for you too. But even if He doesn't, He has already given you His Word. The question is, Are you reading it?

Here's what happened after Abraham expressed his faltering faith:

> And behold, the word of the Lord came to him: "This man shall not be your heir; your very own son

shall be your heir." And he brought him outside and said, "Look toward heaven, and number the stars, if you are able to number them." Then he said to him, "So shall your offspring be." And he believed the LORD, and he counted it to him as righteousness.
—GENESIS 15:4–6

Abraham was struggling to believe, but God spoke to him. He gave him His word. And Abraham believed God, and it was credited to him as righteousness.

We need to examine our hearts. Do we trust God? Do we have unwavering faith, or is it tossed to and fro based on circumstances? If your faith is faltering, you need the Word of the Lord. It's right there for you whenever you need it.

BORN AGAIN

As we saw in chapter 1, when it comes to faith, there is a tension between the natural and the spiritual. To understand faith, you have to understand the kingdom. That is why Jesus said, "You must be born again" (John 3:7, CSB). You can't understand the kingdom unless you are born again.

Born again. That phrase is so simple, yet so profound.

Being born again means you accept Jesus Christ as Lord and Savior. You accept that He shed His blood to cover your sins. And that acceptance has to be real. It can't just be lip service.

When you are born in the natural, there are lots of things you have to learn as you grow. You learn to roll over, crawl, walk, run, and skip. You learn to wash your face, brush your teeth, and comb your hair. You learn to read and write. You are continually learning as you grow.

The same thing happens when you are spiritually born,

when you are born again. You have all kinds of things to learn as you grow. But when you are born again, there are also things that you have to unlearn. No matter your age when you get saved, the world has put a vision into you of how things should be and function, whether it was through television, movies, social media, or any other method the enemy uses to entice you. That's all the stuff you need to unlearn, and it takes some time. And you also need to then learn what God says. You need to put God's vision of how things should be and function into your heart and mind.

That process can be difficult, especially for adults. When you have been living according to the world's standards for so long, it can be hard to accept that you are a spiritual baby starting over with the learning process. It's that tension between the natural and faith, between the flesh and the spirit. That is why you need to be discipled. You get born again, and the process of unlearning and learning continues as you grow.

To move in faith, you have to move in the direction of something that may be scary because you don't know the outcome. And don't forget that the enemy is going to come with his lies, trying to make you believe life without Jesus is better than life with Him. The enemy is going to try to entice you back into bondage by dangling the carrot of comfort—but your bondage wasn't comfortable; you just got used to it.

The apostle Paul wrote,

> But one thing I do: Forgetting what is behind and reaching forward to what is ahead, I pursue as my goal the prize promised by God's heavenly call in Christ Jesus. Therefore, let all of us who are mature

> think this way. And if you think differently about anything, God will reveal this also to you.
> —Philippians 3:13–15, csb

Growing in faith means learning to forget what is behind and instead pursuing the call of God for your life. Think of a runner. Let's say he fell in his last race or lost the biggest race of the year or something similar. For the runner to race well, he can't focus on his fall. He can't focus on his loss. He needs to focus on what is ahead. He can't be looking at the runners beside him. He definitely can't be looking at the runners behind him. He needs to keep his eyes on the prize.

God wants to heal the part of your heart that wants to dwell on the past. He wants you to accept His forgiveness, accept His grace and mercy, accept that His promises are true, and accept that He has a good plan for your life. He wants you to continue to press toward the goal, knowing He will protect you. God is with you. God will never leave you or forsake you.

Keeping your eyes on the prize is a mark of a mature believer. If you allow the enemy to get your eyes off Jesus and on your past, on what you know, on what you feel, you will miss what God wants to show you. You will miss the supernatural. How much of God's truth you are willing to accept affects the rate at which you'll grow.

Spiritual growth is a process, and it doesn't stop. It's called the salvation of your soul. The apostle Peter wrote, "Though you do not now see him, you believe in him and rejoice with joy that is inexpressible and filled with glory, obtaining the outcome of your faith, the salvation of your souls" (1 Pet. 1:8–9). Spiritual growth is constantly pulling you out of something and into something else, out of the world and into the kingdom. It's unlearning and learning, taking out lies and putting in truth, and transforming you into the image of Christ—from faith to faith and glory to glory. Every time you move by faith, it keeps maturing you.

You get saved in an instant. You confess with your mouth that Jesus is Lord, you believe in your heart that God raised Him from the dead, and boom—you're born again. But that is just the first step of faith. Then the sanctification work begins; the discipleship begins.

Sanctification is the process of purifying you, making you holy, consecrating you, and setting you apart for God. Sanctification is also preparation—preparation for the supernatural. Before the children of Israel crossed the Jordan River into the Promised Land (once again, God parted the waters for Israel to cross over on dry ground), Joshua told them, "Sanctify yourselves, for tomorrow the LORD will do wonders among you" (Josh. 3:5, NKJV).

Sanctification is a constant process of dealing with your mind, will, and emotions. It's dealing with the way you think, your desires, and your feelings. And sanctification happens through the Word of God. Jesus prayed, "Sanctify them in the truth; your word is truth" (John 17:17).

When I first started my journey of faith and something was messed up, I would ask myself, "Why am I feeling this way?" And then I would ask, "What desire caused me to feel that way?" Then I would ask myself, "What kind of thinking created that desire?" Then I would take the thought to the Word of God and get it to align with what God says. I did it backward. We need to start with our thoughts. Our thoughts are the source of our desires, our feelings, and our emotions. We can't deal with sinful desires and feelings unless we deal with the thoughts behind them.

Second Corinthians 10:5 says, "We destroy arguments and every lofty opinion raised against the knowledge of God, and take every thought captive to obey Christ." Taking every thought captive to the obedience of Christ is a spiritual discipline. It is not automatic when we get born again. It is a discipline we need to cultivate as we grow up in faith. But when you cultivate that discipline, taking every thought captive to the obedience of Christ starts to become automatic. It's like brushing your teeth. When you were a baby, your parents brushed your teeth for you. Then as a child you did it yourself, but you had to be reminded to do it. But as an adult, brushing your teeth is automatic. You don't have to think about it; you just do it as part of your routine.

Taking every thought captive is changing the way you think. You are a citizen of the kingdom of God, and you need kingdom thinking.

Mustard Seed

The supernatural is about building the kingdom of God, and that starts in you, for Jesus said, "The kingdom of God is within you" (Luke 17:21, NKJV). The Jews of Jesus' day expected the kingdom of God to be a future political, earthly kingdom. But Jesus redefined the kingdom of God as a present spiritual reality. It is not a location on a map that can be observed. It is within the hearts of those who follow Christ. That is why I always say you need to work on your inside. Some people would rather look the part than do that, but they are missing out on this beautiful thing called the kingdom of God. The supernatural nature of God's kingdom transcends human expectation and is at work in you, even when you can't see it.

When Jesus said, "The kingdom of God is within you," it was not too long after the disciples had asked Him to increase their faith, to which He responded, "If you had faith like a grain of mustard seed, you could say to this mulberry tree, 'Be uprooted and planted in the sea,' and it would obey you" (Luke 17:6). Jesus also said, "What is the kingdom of God like? And to what shall I compare it? It is like a grain of mustard seed that a man took and sowed in his garden, and it grew and became a tree, and the birds of the air made nests in its branches" (Luke 13:18–19).

The disciples thought they needed more faith. But they were wrong. They didn't need more faith—they needed more truth. Jesus said even the tiniest amount of faith is enough—because when aligned with the will of God, the tiniest amount of faith will produce miraculous results. That is the supernatural nature of faith. It isn't about the size of your faith; it's about the power of the One you put your faith in. God empowers faith.

The mustard seed is small and seems insignificant. But faith the size of a mustard seed can move mountains when God's behind it. It's a reminder that God uses what seems crazy in the world's eyes to accomplish His will. Remember, Jesus is into the little things.

Because we're people who tend to look only at what's going on outside, we sometimes miss what God is doing on the inside of our hearts. Faith is also a seed that will grow. When we sow the seed of faith and the kingdom of God in our hearts, when we uproot the weeds of doubt and fear and condemnation and shame and all the other lies the devil feeds us, when we water the seed in our hearts with the water of the Word, our faith will grow.

However, I think we hinder our own growth sometimes because we dismiss the mustard seeds as too small to be of importance. We miss the depth of the supernatural in our lives, and we aren't thankful for the little things because we're waiting for someone to get out of a wheelchair.

Luke 17 also tells the story of ten lepers who were healed. But only one of the ten lepers returned to thank Jesus for his healing. Only one gave glory to God. So we often receive God's crazy blessings, but we fail to recognize them as supernatural. We fail to give glory to God for the mustard seeds. Gratitude and recognition of God's work in our lives are important. Gratitude helps growth.

So be thankful for your mustard seed. When that tiny amount of faith gets behind the will of God, you can expect to see the supernatural. And if your heart is good soil, you can also expect that seed to grow and bear fruit, taking territory for the kingdom of God.

Do You Believe?

There was a famous tightrope walker who strung a rope across Niagara Falls. He asked the crowd if they believed he could walk across. The crowd enthusiastically said yes. He walked across and back successfully. Then he asked if they believed he could push a wheelbarrow across. Again, they said yes. He pushed a wheelbarrow across. Finally, he asked if they believed he could push the wheelbarrow across with someone in it. The crowd shouted yes. Then he asked for a volunteer. No one stepped forward. Even though they said they believed, no one believed enough to put their belief into action.

True faith means trusting God completely. True faith is demonstrated not just in words but in action. True faith means believing in God's promises and character even when it requires taking a step of faith.

The truth is that just believing is not faith. James 2:19 says, "You believe that God is one; you do well. Even the demons believe—and shudder!" Faith follows up belief with action. The Book of James also says, "Faith by itself, if it does not have works, is dead" (2:17). Faith is belief that gets moving.

When I talk to people who are struggling, I often ask them some questions: "Do you believe Moses parted the Red Sea so the children of Israel could walk through on dry land when their enemies were chasing them?"

They of course respond, "Yes."

"Do you believe that Jesus was resurrected?"

"Of course."

"Do you believe Jesus used a few loaves and fish to feed a crowd of thousands?"

"Definitely."

"Do you believe that when Paul and Silas worshipped in a prison cell, an earthquake opened the prison doors and unlocked their chains?"

"Yes!"

"Do you believe Jesus raised Lazarus from the dead?"

"Absolutely!"

"So why don't you believe God can help you get some tires for your car so you can get to church?"

Crickets...

When you truly believe, you are going to wind up living a little differently.

The issue so often is that people don't really believe deep down in their hearts. Or they are living under a stronghold of condemnation, guilt, or rejection, so while they 100 percent believe that God did everything I mentioned, they don't believe God will do it for them. Satan has convinced them to believe his lies. Satan gets them to believe the lie that "God can do that, but He can't do this." But the truth is that "with God all things are possible" (Matt. 19:26). Satan steals their peace by making them think that things will never work out for them, but the truth is "all things work together for good to those who love God, to those who are the called according to His purpose" (Rom. 8:28, NKJV). Satan kills their joy by feeding them the lie that they will always be carrying around the baggage from their past like an unbearably heavy load, but the truth is that "if anyone is in Christ, he is a new creation; old things have passed away; behold, all things have become new" (2 Cor. 5:17, NKJV). Satan destroys their hope with the lie that they will never succeed in fulfilling the plans and purposes of God for their life, but the truth is that they "can do all things through Christ who strengthens [them]" (Phil. 4:13, NKJV).

You need to believe the Word, and you can only do that by faith.

You need to believe the Word by faith, and your beliefs also need to line up with the Word. This is a key thing. It's like with "name it and claim it." The concept behind it is true. Jesus said, "Ask whatever you want and it will be done for you," but the first part of that verse says, "If you remain in me and my words remain in you…" (John 15:7, CSB). And Jesus said, "For I have come down from heaven, not to do my own will, but the will of him who sent me" (John 6:38, CSB). Jesus came to do the will of the Father. He talked about it over and over again. Again, He also said, "But seek first the kingdom of God and his righteousness, and all these things will be provided for you" (Matt. 6:33, CSB).

When we start chasing things instead of Jesus, it's like we are saying Jesus is not enough. We think if we don't have "all these things," then God's not doing His job. But God's things and "all these things" are totally different. God's more concerned with your character than with your comfort. All His treasures are kingdom treasures. So when Jesus said, "Ask whatever you want," He wasn't saying to treat God like a piñata or a genie in a lamp.

Do I attribute everything that God has done in my life to God? Absolutely. Anything good in me is there because God placed it in me. Everything I have is because God gave it to me. But I'm not seeking the things; I'm seeking the kingdom. I'm seeking authentic relationship with Jesus every day. He gives me ideas, He connects me with people, and He does everything He needs to do for me to continue fulfilling my purpose. And in the midst of that everybody somehow gets blessed. But the blessings are not at the forefront. When we seek the added things before the kingdom, we are going outside the will of God.

I believe the enemy has used concepts like "name it and claim it" to distort the Word and the will of God. That distortion gets people frustrated, and it can cause them to fall away. It can cause them to lose their faith because God isn't a genie in a lamp.

Do I believe that you can hear it, accept it, and God makes it grow? Absolutely. When that happens, you're speaking and confessing, and you're coming into agreement with the Word of God. Luke 18:27 says, "What is impossible with man is possible with God" (CSB). While I was studying that verse, I looked up the word *impossible* because I felt in my spirit like God wanted me to. One dictionary defines *impossible* as "not able to occur, exist, or be done."[2]

I believe what we've done is that when we look at Luke 18:27 through our Western eyes, with that definition of *impossible* in our minds, we start thinking of things that are not able to occur and assuming God will make them occur. I think we often view that verse from a place of selfishness. We combine that with Matthew 21:22 (CSB)—"And if you believe, you will receive whatever you ask for in prayer"—and we come up with this wish list for God. We start thinking that just because we think it's going to happen, it's going to happen. Believe, receive; believe, receive; believe, receive.

But if we think that, we've missed it. We've missed the will of God. We've missed the will of the Father. The context of Luke 18:27 is Jesus had just said, "How hard it is for those who have wealth to enter the kingdom of God! For it is easier for a camel to go through the eye of a needle than for a rich person to enter the kingdom of God." Then someone asked Him, "Then who can be saved?" That's when Jesus said, "What is impossible with man is possible with God" (Luke 18:24–27, CSB). The person asking Jesus the question was thinking He meant that it was impossible for a rich person to be saved. But that doesn't line up with the will of the Father, who is "not wanting any to perish but all to come to repentance" (2 Pet. 3:9, CSB). So it isn't impossible for a rich person to be saved. "What is impossible with man is possible with God." And think about this—a camel can go through the eye of a needle if the camel is in a state of brokenness. "The sacrifices of God are a broken spirit;

a broken and contrite heart, O God, you will not despise" (Ps. 51:17). You can receive the impossible, but the impossible is done according to the will and the Word of God.

Living by Faith

The apostle Paul acknowledged the natural human inclination to rely on what is visible and tangible. However, he called believers to rise above this inclination, grounding their lives in the invisible and eternal truths of God. In 2 Corinthians 5:7 Paul captured the essence of the Christian walk: living by faith, not by sight. This call invites us to place our trust in God's invisible hand guiding our lives, to prioritize eternal truths over temporary circumstances, and to embrace the hope of what is unseen.

I've heard it said many times that the opposite of faith is fear. But whenever I hear that, my mind goes to 2 Corinthians 5:7. I believe, biblically, that the opposite of faith is sight. In that verse Paul didn't say, "We walk by faith, not by fear." He said, "We walk by faith, not by sight." The opposite of faith is sight.

Sight refers to what we physically see. But *sight* also can refer to mental perception. When Paul said we don't walk by sight, he was referring to our limited human perspective and understanding. The problem with walking by sight is that many times our human perception or understanding of what is happening in our lives or in the world is clouded by fear, doubt, or worldly values. And all that can lead to anxiety, depression, indecision, and more. When you are walking by sight, you are operating out of what the human mind can see. You see all the chaos going on in the world, and you get afraid because you are going off what you know or what world the tells you rather than the Word of God, the knowledge of God, and the revelation God has given you. While fear isn't the opposite of faith, when you are consumed by fear, it is a pretty clear indication you are not walking by faith.

Walking by faith is vital. It is impossible to please God without faith. As I said before, true faith means trusting God completely, not just in words but in action. True faith means believing God's promises are true. True faith means your decisions, your actions, and your priorities are guided by trust in God. True faith means embracing God's will even when it contradicts our understanding or desires. True faith means trusting in God's character, that He is who He says He is:

> The Lord, the Lord, a God merciful and gracious, slow to anger, and abounding in steadfast love and faithfulness, keeping steadfast love for thousands, forgiving iniquity and transgression and sin.
> —Exodus 34:6–7

> I am your shield, your exceedingly great reward.
> —Genesis 15:1, nkjv

> Fear not, for I am with you; be not dismayed, for I am your God; I will strengthen you, I will help you, I will uphold you with my righteous right hand.
> —Isaiah 41:10

> I am the bread of life; whoever comes to me shall not hunger, and whoever believes in me shall never thirst.
> —John 6:35

> I am the light of the world. Whoever follows me will not walk in darkness, but will have the light of life.
> —John 8:12

> I am the good shepherd. I know my own and my own know me.
> —John 10:14

One of the other things God said about Himself is "I am the Lord, your healer" (Exod. 15:26). I believe that God wants to heal the physical form. I also believe He wants to heal the emotional form. There is a form of emotionalism where you're like a roller coaster, racing between highs and lows, taking sharp curves, and sometimes even turning upside down. You let your feelings lead you, and you end up in a mess because your feelings led you wrong. Only then do you want to be led by faith.

Feelings aren't a bad thing. They just indicate what's happening in your heart. But you're never to be led by your feelings. They aren't reliable, and they are just going to put you back on the roller coaster. Get off the roller coaster. You need to be led by your faith. You need to walk by faith. You need to live by faith.

Remember, James 1:2–4 says, "Count it all joy, my brothers, when you meet trials of various kinds, for you know that the testing of your faith produces steadfastness. And let steadfastness have its full effect, that you may be perfect and complete, lacking in nothing." The apostle James had some good news and some bad news for us. The bad news is you are going to face all kinds of trials. You are going to face physical, emotional, spiritual, financial, and relational challenges. Your faith is going to be tested.

For the believer it's not a question of if but when these various trials and the testing of your faith will happen—because they will happen.

Oh, but there is also good news. "The testing of your faith produces steadfastness." Other translations say the testing of your faith produces "patience," "perseverance," or "endurance" (NKJV, CJB, CSB). This is so good. Trials serve as a test of faith, and that test refines and strengthens our faith. It's like gold or silver being purified. Psalm 66:10 says, "For you, God, tested us; you refined us as silver is refined" (CSB). When metals like silver and gold are refined, the ore is placed over the fire where the flames are hottest, causing the metal to liquefy and the impurities, or dross, to rise to the top. The dross is removed, and the process is repeated until the smith can see himself in the silver or gold.

The Bible actually refers to God as a refiner's fire (Mal. 3:2). God doesn't refine us to hurt us. It is part of the sanctification process. He is trying to help us get rid of all the junk we are carrying around like a bunch of heavy burdens.

When you have an authentic, intimate relationship with the Lord, He refines you. He changes you. He purifies you. He sanctifies you. Yes, the tests, trials, and suffering are uncomfortable. No one likes it when things heat up. But every time things heat up and God removes a layer of dross, God can see more of Jesus in you: "We all, with unveiled faces, are looking as in a mirror at the glory of the Lord and are being transformed into the same image from glory to glory; this is from the Lord who is the Spirit" (2 Cor. 3:18, CSB).

When you are living by faith, you will develop an

intimate relationship with God. The apostle Paul wrote, "My goal is to know him and the power of his resurrection and the fellowship of his sufferings" (Phil. 3:10, CSB). Why is that important? Because a lot of times, we look at intimacy with God as simply knowing about Him. But that isn't intimacy. That isn't an authentic relationship. You can know about someone without actually knowing them. To have intimacy with someone, you have to actually know them. You have to get close to them. You have to draw near. When you move by faith and draw near to that refining fire, the fire begins to burn. When you draw near to God, He draws near to you, and it cleanses you and purifies you (Jas. 4:8). God does the supernatural in you.

When you live by faith, when your faith is tested and you come out refined on the other side, something else happens: "You rejoice in this, even though now for a short time, if necessary, you suffer grief in various trials so that the proven character of your faith—more valuable than gold which, though perishable, is refined by fire—may result in praise, glory, and honor at the revelation of Jesus Christ" (1 Pet. 1:6–7, CSB). After you are refined, your faith is more valuable than gold, and it brings praise, glory, and honor to Jesus.

Defeating Doubt and Fear

I think when we operate out of sight, it causes doubt and fear. When we operate in faith, it defeats doubt and fear.

When you are walking in true faith, you are also walking in humility. I believe when you're moving in humility, that's the fear of the Lord because you're allowing the

Move-a-Mountain Faith

Holy Spirit to counsel you based on the truth of God's Word, which has the final authority. When you move in pride, you're allowing the enemy to counsel you with lies.

Sometimes we question why it's such a big deal to follow worldly wisdom rather than godly wisdom. Worldly wisdom is still wisdom, right? Wrong. Human logic that goes against the Word of God isn't wisdom. Advice from the world that contradicts Scripture isn't wisdom. Wisdom that denies the truth is not wisdom. Remember, the devil is the father of lies, and his goal is to steal, kill, and destroy. That is why the Book of James says that "such wisdom does not come down from above but is earthly, unspiritual, demonic" (3:15, CSB).

At times, we think only things like drinking, drugs, and extramarital sex are demonic, but the devil has a lot more things than just those in his arsenal. He wants you to take worldly advice about your marriage that will end up destroying it. He wants you to accept demonic counsel from the world about raising your kids so he can steal them. When you aren't accepting the counsel of the Father, you are being manipulated by the enemy.

The enemy's counsel will give you vain imagination. It will cause you to fear. It will cause you to doubt. It will cause you to walk by sight rather than faith—and the things he puts in your sight may not even be real.

Have you ever watched a scary movie? You know it isn't real, but when something particularly scary happens, you jump out of your skin, or you scream, or you might even cover your eyes. It doesn't matter that it isn't real. The director of the movie used imagination to manipulate your feelings. The things you see on the screen aren't real, but your fear is real. The enemy uses the same kinds of tricks. He creates worry in the form of meditation on a negative story. He spins this story and makes it so big and real that you actually believe it. We sometimes get mad at Adam and Eve for buying into the devil's lies and biting the apple, but the truth is we often do the same thing. The devil creates this dramatic story that causes us to doubt God, and we bite.

Deception is not caused by lies. It's caused by your belief in those lies. That means you bite the apple, and instead of spitting out the lies, you swallow them. You digest them. You allow them to feed your thoughts, which in turn feed your desires and emotions.

You overcome fear and doubt with faith. First John 5:4 says, "Everyone who has been born of God conquers the world. This is the victory that has conquered the world: our faith" (CSB). Faith is how you conquer fear and doubt. Faith is how you overcome the obstacles. Faith is how you move a mountain. Faith is how you defeat the enemy. Faith is how you achieve victory. If you are struggling with fear, anxiety, and doubt, it is time to stop walking by sight and start walking by faith.

And remember, "if you have faith the size of a mustard seed, you will tell this mountain, 'Move from here to there,' and it will move. Nothing will be impossible for you" (Matt. 17:20, CSB).

Chapter 6
WATER OF THE WORD

When people say, "I don't have time to read the Word," I say, "You're not following Jesus—because Jesus is the Word." And Jesus isn't just the Logos. He's the rhema—the living Word.

Our tendency is to quote, "Man shall not live by bread alone, but by every word that comes from the mouth of God" (Matt. 4:4), but then all we eat is bread. Remember, when Jesus said, "Man shall not live by bread alone, but by every word that comes from the mouth of God," He didn't turn the stones into loaves of bread. He actually lived out the Word. He took the written Word of God—the Logos—and turned it into the sword of the Spirit, which is a rhema word, and used it to defeat the devil. If Jesus, who is the Word, used the Word and experienced the supernatural, how much more do we need the Word if we want to experience the supernatural in our lives.

Daily Bread

Matthew 4:4 changed my life. It opened my eyes to the power of the Word of God. It also opened my eyes to the authority of the Word.

The Word of God holds supreme authority. It's pre-eminent, meaning it is of paramount importance. The authority of the Word comes from Jesus because He is the Word: "In the beginning was the Word, and the Word was with God, and the Word was God....The Word became flesh and dwelt among us" (John 1:1, 14).

Jesus demonstrated His authority and the authority of the written Word of God when the devil tempted Him in the wilderness. Jesus had been fasting for forty days and forty nights. He was hungry. The lack of food had weakened Him physically. The devil knew this and went on the attack. But Jesus was able to defend against each and every attack by using the Word of God. He was tempted, just like we are, but He was victorious over the temptation because He knew the inherent power and authority in the Word of God. He may not have had bread, but He had the Word, and the Word was more than enough to sustain Him.

There was a time in my life when I had nothing. I had just gotten out of prison. I was all alone in Texas. There were no finances coming in. I felt like I was at a crossroads, and I was going through a battle, trying to figure out which direction to go.

The enemy attacked. The father of lies did what he does best. The devil was telling me things like, "The worst thing that happened is you went to jail. Jail wasn't that bad. Look at you. You have nothing. Why not go back to your old life? At least then you had something," and, "This is the God you serve? You have no money. You're alone and abandoned. Why are you still serving Him?" The enemy knew exactly what to say, and he was shouting it at me.

I had a choice. I could go down the road toward my old life, my old ways, and my old issues—the road toward

Water of the Word

bondage, both physical and spiritual—or I could go down the road to new life, new ways, and a new start—the road toward freedom and abundant life. Then I heard this whisper that said, "Do you trust Me?" In the midst of the battle I heard the still, small voice. God was fulfilling His promise: "And your ears shall hear a word behind you, saying, 'This is the way, walk in it,' when you turn to the right or when you turn to the left" (Isa. 30:21).

I opened up the Bible and started reading. I also got a bunch of Christian books and started reading a little bit of each one of them. It was the only thing I knew to do. It was the only way I knew how to fight against the devil and his temptations and lies. But it got me through to the next thing during a hard season.

A little while later, a lady from Memphis, Tennessee, called. She wanted me to come share my testimony. It was my first assignment after I got out of prison. It was just a short assignment. It was just a little thing, but Jesus is into the little things, and He used it in my life in a big way.

I had never met the lady before, but God gave her a word for me. She said, "The Lord is telling me to tell you to read Deuteronomy 8."

As I mentioned in chapter 2, Deuteronomy 8 contains a passage Jesus quoted when the devil was tempting Him in the wilderness, and it covers so much more than not living by bread alone:

> Remember that the LORD your God led you on the entire journey these forty years in the wilderness, so that he might humble you and test you to know what was in your heart, whether or not you would keep his commands. He humbled you by letting you

> go hungry; then he gave you manna to eat, which you and your ancestors had not known, so that you might learn that man does not live on bread alone but on every word that comes from the mouth of the Lord....Keep in mind that the Lord your God has been disciplining you just as a man disciplines his son. So keep the commands of the Lord your God by walking in his ways and fearing him. For the Lord your God is bringing you into a good land....
>
> Be careful that you don't forget the Lord your God by failing to keep his commands, ordinances, and statutes that I am giving you today. When you eat and are full, and build beautiful houses to live in, and your herds and flocks grow large, and your silver and gold multiply, and everything else you have increases, be careful that your heart doesn't become proud and you forget the Lord your God who brought you out of the land of Egypt, out of the place of slavery.
>
> —Deuteronomy 8:2–3, 5–7, 11–14, csb

During that difficult season, the first thing I learned is that man does not live by bread alone but by every word that proceeds from the mouth of God. I may not have had anything in the eyes of the world, but God had already given me everything I needed to live—and not only live but thrive in an abundant life of freedom.

I realized that any change in my life was God doing a supernatural work in me. God was humbling me and helping me learn how to live off Jesus rather than pursuing "all these things"—food and drink, clothes, shelter, and so on. He was teaching me to not worry and instead seek Him: "Don't worry about your life, what you will eat or what you will drink; or about your body, what you will wear....Your heavenly Father knows that you need them. But seek first the kingdom of God and his righteousness, and all these things will be provided for you" (Matt. 6:25, 32–33, csb).

When the devil tempted Jesus, he was trying to get Him to focus on His physical needs. Jesus used the Word because He lived off the Word, and in my life God was teaching me how to do the same thing.

Sometimes we complain because we think everything supernatural is shiny and spectacular. But supernatural things are often small and simple. There may have been things in the natural that I didn't have, but God was providing shelter and food, and He was sustaining my daily life. He was giving me my daily bread—and that right there is a supernatural act of God. Lots of people miss it because they would rather complain than recognize the supernatural in the daily things of life. They miss the supernatural because they don't realize that God's Word is enough, that it is sufficient for every circumstance.

God's Word is supernatural.

Spillover

When I look at people who have an authentic, intimate, heart-level relationship with Jesus, I see a connection. And out of that connection there's an overflow, a spillover.

You can't have a relationship with Jesus that causes spillover without the Word because Jesus is the Word. Sometimes people are walking according to the ways of the Lord, but they are not grounded in the Word. They are not being washed with the water of the Word. They are not meditating on the Word and mulling it over. They are not renewing their minds with the Word. They are not writing God's Word on their hearts. Then when troubles come, it is all too easy for them to start walking another way—but that way leads only to more troubles.

Jesus said, "I am the way, the truth, and the life. No one comes to the Father except through Me" (John 14:6, MEV). The Greek word for *way* is *hodos*. It means road, way, progress, journey, and a way of thinking, feeling, and deciding.[1] Jesus was saying He is the only road to the Father, but He was also saying, "Look to Me for how to make progress on the journey of your life. I know the truth because I am the truth. I know what the purpose of your life is because I created you and am the source of all life. I know the way you should go, and when you seek Me, I will direct your paths."

The believers in the early church were called men and women "of the Way" (Acts 9:2, MEV). There was something different about the way they lived, the way they loved one another and the lost, the way they walked through life, the way they treated others, and the way they handled suffering and persecution. And their commitment to walking in the ways of the Lord was so strong that they referred to themselves as being "of the Way," and even nonbelievers started doing it too.

But living that way is the fruit of relationship with Jesus. It is the fruit of spending time in His presence and in His Word.

When you have that deep, authentic relationship with Jesus, you start to live that way effortlessly. Stuff starts to spill over. You may miss the mark here and cross a line there, but because of the relationship you have with the

Water of the Word

Lord, the Holy Spirit will get you back on track. God will fulfill the same promise for you that He did for me: "And your ears shall hear a word behind you, saying, 'This is the way, walk in it,' when you turn to the right or when you turn to the left" (Isa. 30:21).

When the spillover happens, you won't struggle to forgive someone, because not forgiving feels weird. You won't need to be told to evangelize; it will just happen as the fruit of what God is doing in your life. You won't open your Bible out of guilt or obligation; you will open it with joy and expectation because you have a hunger for the things of the Lord. Once you reach a certain point in your faith journey, so many supernatural things start to happen naturally. Living out your faith is not something you have to think about.

There is simplicity to the gospel. There is no need to overcomplicate it. Romans 10:9–10 keeps it pretty basic: "If you confess with your mouth the Lord Jesus and believe in your heart that God has raised Him from the dead, you will be saved. For with the heart one believes unto righteousness, and with the mouth confession is made unto salvation" (NKJV). I think the issue some people have is that they confess with their mouths, but they don't believe with their hearts. They try to convince themselves to believe in their minds, but they don't recognize it is a heart issue. Belief starts in your heart.

And here's what is so amazing about your heart: God wants to give you a new one. Everything in life springs from your heart—in the natural and in the supernatural. Ezekiel 36:26 says, "And I will give you a new heart, and a new spirit I will put within you. And I will remove the heart of stone from your flesh and give you a heart of flesh." Once God has given you that new heart, you want to make sure that it stays soft and pliable.

Jesus told a parable to His disciples:

> Listen! Behold, a sower went out to sow. And it happened, as he sowed, that some seed fell by the wayside; and the birds of the air came and devoured it. Some fell on stony ground, where it did not have much earth; and immediately it sprang up because it had no depth of earth. But when the sun was up it was scorched, and because it had no root it withered away. And some seed fell among thorns; and the thorns grew up and choked it, and it yielded no crop. But other seed fell on good ground and yielded a crop that sprang up, increased and produced: some thirtyfold, some sixty, and some a hundred.
> —MARK 4:3–8, NKJV

Jesus later explained the parable to His disciples:

> The sower sows the word. And these are the ones by the wayside where the word is sown. When they hear, Satan comes immediately and takes away the word that was sown in their hearts. These likewise are the ones sown on stony ground who, when they hear the word, immediately receive it with gladness; and they have no root in themselves, and so endure only for a time. Afterward, when tribulation or persecution arises for the word's sake, immediately they stumble. Now these are the ones sown among thorns; they are the ones who hear the word, and the cares of this world, the deceitfulness of riches, and the desires for other things entering in choke the word, and it becomes unfruitful. But these are

> the ones sown on good ground, those who hear the word, accept it, and bear fruit: some thirtyfold, some sixty, and some a hundred.
> —Mark 4:14–20, nkjv

You want your heart to be good ground. You want your heart to be good soil. That means you need to have a receptive heart. You hear the truth and accept it. You hear the truth and choose to believe it in your heart. Your job is simple: Believe. Then God does His job and makes it grow. It's not complicated.

Once you choose to believe, the seed of the Word in your heart will grow. And you can foster that growth by continuing to use the water of the Word in your life:

> Blessed is the man who walks not in the counsel of the wicked, nor stands in the way of sinners, nor sits in the seat of scoffers; but his delight is in the law of the Lord, and on his law he meditates day and night. He is like a tree planted by streams of water that yields its fruit in its season, and its leaf does not wither. In all that he does, he prospers.
> —Psalm 1:1–3

This plays a role in the balance of spirit and truth, of the Spirit and the Word, in your life. You need that balance to fully experience the supernatural in your life.

Renewing Your Mind

If you're not renewing your mind with the Word of God and allowing God to transform you, you are still going to struggle with things like fear, depression, anxiety, and hopelessness, not to mention all the lies the devil has gotten you to believe about yourself. The Bible says, "Do not be conformed to this world, but be transformed by the renewal of your mind, that by testing you may discern what is the will of God, what is good and acceptable and perfect" (Rom. 12:2).

I went to a Christian neurologist to get some information to help people struggling with addiction. The neurologist told me about the part of the brain called the limbic system, which is considered the mind, or the heart (with *heart* meaning your emotional nature rather than the organ that pumps blood through your body). The limbic system is the part of your brain that controls your emotional responses and behavior. Talking to the neurologist was so fascinating. He said that whether you break a leg or break up a relationship, the limbic system registers the pain the same way. Think about that. So whether suffering is physical, emotional, or spiritual, it affects your brain the same way. But that same part of your brain controls your behavior. That is why it is so important to renew your mind.

Suffering is part of life. Nobody really wants to hear that, but that doesn't make it any less true. The apostle Paul, who was well acquainted with suffering, wrote, "For it has been granted to you on Christ's behalf not only to believe in him, but also to suffer for him" (Phil. 1:29, CSB). I think fear of suffering is why some people avoid taking crazy steps of faith. When God asks them to do something that is outside their comfort zone, their minds go down the "what if..." road. But let me tell you, if God is pushing you out of your comfort zone, your comfort zone is no longer the right place for you to be. I don't know about you, but I want to be in the right place, even if it means stepping out of my comfort zone.

And as you mature as a follower of Jesus, you start to realize that suffering is never without purpose. Again, that's why the Word says, "Count it all joy, my brothers, when you meet trials of various kinds" (Jas. 1:2). It also says, "For our momentary light affliction is producing for us an absolutely incomparable eternal weight of glory" (2 Cor. 4:17, CSB). And never forget that God promised "all things work together for the good of those who love God, who are called according to his purpose" (Rom. 8:28, CSB).

That's why we need to renew our minds. We need to change our mindsets to recognize that whatever God is doing in our lives, even if it is painful, is good for us.

My son is a bodybuilder, and he trains others. One day, he said, "Dad, you know what's weird? Most of the time when I'm training somebody, they start complaining. I know they're not doing the calorie intake because I can tell by their body fat and all those numbers, right? They've had five cheat meals when I told them they could have one, and then they complain that they aren't getting the results they want. The interesting part is they're all like, 'When am I going to be able to eat well?' And I'm like, 'You are eating well. If you want results, why do you want to go back to eating junk?'" My son knows that if they don't change their mindsets, they are going to go right back to their old habits, and nothing will ever change.

It's the same with the things of the spirit. If you want to change, if you want to be transformed into the image of Christ from glory to glory, your mindset has to change.

I heard someone say that thought patterns in your brain—in the limbic system—work kind of like cattle trails. Let's say you have a herd of cattle, and you need them to start using a new water source. At first to get the cattle to go to the new watering hole, you are going to have to drive them there. It might not be easy. There might be obstacles in the way, and the cattle will tend to want to go back to the old spot. So you have to keep driving them to the new spot. But over time, a trail develops. And eventually the cattle will go to the new watering hole on their own. They won't have to be driven there anymore.

That's how your brain works. To renew your mind, you have to create new trails. Your old negative and worldly thought patterns have dug themselves down deep in your brain, so it will take time and effort to redirect your thoughts. But every time you take a thought captive to the obedience of Christ, you are starting to develop a new trail. Every time you have a new experience that demonstrates the goodness or faithfulness of God, it develops the trail. Every time you suffer and choose to rejoice and ask God what He is trying to teach you rather than complaining, you develop the trail.

Remember, suffering has a purpose. It is part of the process of sanctification. It hurts, but God is using it to refine you. It's funny—we all love the song "Refiner's Fire," but when it actually comes down to it, we don't like going through the refining fire. It's hot, and it burns. But it is all part of God making us look more and more like Jesus.

The key to renewing your mind is in 2 Corinthians 10:5: "Take every thought captive to obey Christ." You can't control the thoughts that pop into your head, but you can choose what you do with them once they pop in for a visit. When you recognize that a thought doesn't line up with the Word of God, you need to take control of it and get rid of it. And that doesn't mean just thinking, "I'm not going to think that." If that's all you do, you are still thinking it, just in the negative. Instead, you need to replace the thought with the truth. You need to replace the lie with what God says.

For example, let's say the devil pops this old standard into your mind: "Do you honestly think God forgave you for that horrible thing you did? There is no way He would ever forgive you for something like that." You need to choose to replace that thought with the truth, and there are lots of options to choose from, such as the following:

> As far as the east is from the west, so far does he remove our transgressions from us.
> —PSALM 103:12

> If we confess our sins, he is faithful and righteous to forgive us our sins and to cleanse us from all unrighteousness.
> —1 JOHN 1:9, CSB

> In him we have redemption through his blood, the forgiveness of our trespasses, according to the riches of his grace.
> —EPHESIANS 1:7, CSB

The apostle Paul gave some really good advice to the Philippians about taking every thought captive. He wrote, "Finally, brothers, whatever is true, whatever is honorable, whatever is just, whatever is pure, whatever is lovely, whatever is commendable, if there is any excellence, if there is anything worthy of praise, think about these things" (Phil. 4:8). You need to choose to think of things that are true, honorable, just, pure, lovely, commendable, excellent, and praiseworthy. You need to renew your mind by directing your thoughts to those things over and over and over again until eventually a new mindset has been developed.

And just in case you didn't realize it, when your mind is transformed by the washing of the water of the Word of God, it's supernatural.

Study to Show Yourself Approved

Something really hit me one day as I read Hebrews 11:1–2: "Now faith is the reality of what is hoped for, the proof of what is not seen. For by this our ancestors were *approved*" (csb, emphasis added). Other translations of verse 2 say things like "obtained a good report," "received their commendation," or "obtained a good testimony" (kjv, esv, nkjv), but that word *approved* captured my attention. It took me to 2 Timothy 2:15: "Study to show yourself approved by God, a workman who need not be ashamed, rightly dividing the word of truth" (mev). A long time ago some guy asked me a question about 2 Timothy 2:15: "Study for what?" I didn't know how to answer his question.

God later gave me the answer while I was preaching one day, and He connected these two Bible passages for me. Hebrews 11:2 says our ancestors were approved because of their faith. They were approved because they moved by faith in the things that God was telling them to do.

Now, I study the Word of God so I can know God. When I know Him, I know what He sounds like. When I know what He sounds like, I recognize His voice when He speaks to me. When I recognize His voice when He speaks to me, I can move by faith, even if He is telling

Water of the Word

me to do something that seems crazy to my human logic. When I move by faith, I am approved.

So study for what? Study to be approved! Study the Word so you know God, so you know what He sounds like, so you recognize His voice, so you can move by faith, and so that you get approved!

You move by faith in God. You move by faith in the Word. Faith moves. If you just read the Scripture without the Spirit and are not willing to live it out, you aren't moving in faith. Studying the Scriptures isn't about stuffing your head with a bunch of facts about the Bible. It's about getting to know the Word so you can know the living Word. It's about developing an intimate relationship with God.

When the Jews were seeking to kill Jesus because He healed on the Sabbath, He told them, "You don't have his word residing in you, because you don't believe the one he sent. You pore over the Scriptures because you think you have eternal life in them, and yet they testify about me. But you are not willing to come to me so that you may have life" (John 5:38–40, CSB). Reading the Word just for the sake of reading it is not enough. Studying for the sake of studying is not going to cut it. Reading and studying and meditating on the Word is about getting to know Jesus, and when you have that heart-level relationship with Him, you are going to live out the Word by faith—not out of obligation or guilt but out of love for the One who gave you life.

Magnifying Glass or Mirror?

James 1:22–25 (CSB) says,

> But be doers of the word and not hearers only, deceiving yourselves. Because if anyone is a hearer of

the word and not a doer, he is like someone looking at his own face in a mirror. For he looks at himself, goes away, and immediately forgets what kind of person he was. But the one who looks intently into the perfect law of freedom and perseveres in it, and is not a forgetful hearer but a doer who works—this person will be blessed in what he does.

You hear the Word every Sunday. You hear the Word on Facebook reels. You hear the Word on all those YouTube channels you follow. You hear the Word over and over, but if all you do is hear it, and you never do it, you are deceiving yourself. You're like the Jews that Jesus said didn't have the Word abiding in them. You think you're fine and all is well, but you are missing out. You are missing out on an authentic relationship with Jesus. You are missing out on abundant life. You are missing out on walking in freedom. You are missing out on the supernatural.

The Bible is a mirror.

When I'm doing marriage mediation, I tell couples that when a test, a trial, or trouble comes, they have two choices: magnifying glass or mirror. The magnifying glass is the pride side, the side where you are hyperfocused on the flaws and foibles of the other person. I've said it before, and I'll say it again: When you choose to walk in pride, you are being counseled by the enemy. Whether you are dealing with an issue in your marriage or any other issue, being counseled by the enemy of your soul is never a wise choice.

The enemy wants you to use a magnifying glass. He wants you to examine others, looking for their sins and shortcomings, their mistakes and mess-ups. He wants you to use the Word as a weapon against other people rather than as a weapon against him. He wants you to do things your way instead of God's way. If he can keep you focused on others, he will keep you from seeing what God is trying to do in you. Taking territory for the kingdom starts inside you, but that will never happen if you never examine yourself. So when an issue comes up and you initially get prideful, you are playing right into the devil's hands.

That's why I tell married couples they need to drop the magnifying glass and pick up the mirror. The mirror is the humility side. When you pick up the mirror, you are asking, "What is God saying to *me*? Where am *I* out of alignment with the Word?" When you look in the mirror of the Word of God in humility, you are allowing the Holy Spirit to refine you, to sanctify you, to transform you, and to make you more like Jesus.

The goal is not to go to the mirror of the Word after you have an argument or after you mess up or miss the mark. The goal is to hide the Word in your heart so you realize you are out of alignment before you have an argument or before you mess up or miss the mark. Psalm 119:11 says, "Your word I have hidden in my heart, that I might not sin against You" (NKJV). The goal is to take what you see in the mirror of the Word and apply it. The goal is to bring the truth of the Word into your reality. The goal is to obey out of love rather than disobey and ask for forgiveness, or obey out of fear.

That doesn't mean you can't ask God for forgiveness when you mess up. You should do that, and God will forgive you. He is abounding in grace. But our goal should be to not sin in the first place. The apostle Paul wrote,

> Should we continue in sin so that grace may multiply? Absolutely not! How can we who died to sin

> still live in it?...Therefore do not let sin reign in your mortal body, so that you obey its desires. And do not offer any parts of it to sin as weapons for unrighteousness. But as those who are alive from the dead, offer yourselves to God, and all the parts of yourselves to God as weapons for righteousness. For sin will not rule over you, because you are not under the law but under grace.
> —Romans 6:1–2, 12–14, csb

The other side of that is the motive of our obedience. God wants us to obey Him out of love, not out of fear.

I have messed up a ton as a parent. I admit that openly. But there is one thing I know I got right. I remember telling my son Josh, "I don't want you to ever listen to us because you're afraid of the punishment. I just want you to listen to us because you love us when you're out there."

When the motive is love, it changes how a person listens. When the motive is love, it changes how a person obeys. Jesus said, "If you love me, you will keep my commands" (John 14:15, csb). He didn't say, "If you are afraid of Me" or "If you don't want to get punished" or "Because I'm shaking My finger at you..." He said, "If you love Me..." It was gentle. It was humble. It was the act of a good Father who loves His kids and wants them to obey out of love.

Looking in the mirror is pointless if you don't use it to fix what's wrong. If you look in the mirror and see something green in your teeth, are you going to walk away without getting it out? If you look in the mirror and see that your shirt is misbuttoned, are you just going to walk around like that all day? If you look in the mirror and see that your hair is all messed up, are you just going go about your business without fixing it? You wouldn't do that, and you shouldn't be doing that with the mirror of the Word either.

God has given us His Word as an amazing gift. God's Word is "profitable for teaching, for rebuking, for correcting, for training in righteousness" (2 Tim. 3:16, CSB). But you have to accept it. You have to apply it. You have to do it. You have to walk it out by faith. And you do all those things not out of guilt or fear or shame but out of love for the Lord. You do it because the relationship you have with Jesus makes you want to please Him; you want to be approved. And remember, every time you read the Word, every time you apply the Word, every time you meditate on the Word, every time you hide the Word in your heart, you are experiencing the supernatural because God promised, "So shall my word be that goes out from my mouth; it shall not return to me empty, but it shall accomplish that which I purpose, and shall succeed in the thing for which I sent it" (Isa. 55:11).

Chapter 7
THE POWER OF PRAYER

Jesus said, "Whenever you pray..." (Matt. 6:5, csb). I just love that *whenever*. It's not an *if*. It means there is the expectation that you pray. Jesus is assuming that if you are a believer, if you have a relationship with God, then you have a prayer life. It also means that Jesus wants to talk to you. He wants to have a conversation with you. He wants to have a heart-to-heart with you so you can share with Him and He can share with you.

Prayer is about many things, but ultimately it is about cooperating with God to bring about His plan, not trying to bend Him to your will. When you don't pray, you will grow distant from God. When you do pray, you will not only grow closer to God but also become more like Him because you will be sensitive to what He values most.

When I think about prayer, I think about an exchange. I think about a conversation. Sometimes we think prayer is only effective when it is out loud and we are engaging in spiritual warfare. There is definitely a place for that. There is definitely a place for confessing, for coming into agreement with what the Father has to say. But there is also a place for the internal, heart-to-heart conversations with

Jesus. I have conversations with the Lord all day long, but many of them are not out loud. They are just in my heart and mind. At one time, I thought, "Man, am I doing this wrong?" But God just wants to talk with you. It doesn't matter whether it is out loud.

Prayer is a time to commune with God so He can share what heaven has for you. This is why filling your heart with the Word matters. When I commune with God, and I'm meditating on and even wrestling with a passage of Scripture, I'm talking to God as a friend because He wants to share things with me. He wants me to understand His Word, His heart, His vision, His plan, and His will. He wants to give me revelation.

Prayer is a conversation. It's a dialogue, not a monologue. That means I need to say, "Holy Spirit, what are You saying to me?" I'm not just talking. I'm also listening.

I've had to practice active listening in my life, especially because I'm a talker. But it's not just about me doing all the talking. Yes, when I'm preaching, I'm doing all the talking, but at other times, I still listen to my wife. I listen to my kids. But I have been practicing a different way of listening for a couple of years now. When you are talking to me, I'm not just hearing the words that are coming out of your mouth. I'm not just letting your words go in one ear and out the other. When you are talking and I'm listening, I'm actively participating in what your heart is saying. "Out of the abundance of the heart his mouth speaks" (Luke 6:45). Your words are telling me what is in your heart. When I get to know your heart, I know how to serve you better.

God's words reveal His heart. The Bible is not just words on pages. E. M. Bounds writes, "The Word of God is the food by which prayer is nourished and made strong."[1] The

Word is a revelation of the heart of God because He wants you to know Him. He wants you to know His nature, His character. When we listen to what God is saying, when we commune with Him in prayer and hear His heart through His Word, it enables us to better serve Him and also to better participate in the wonders He is doing in the world. When you understand God's heart, it deepens your relationship with Him. Connection happens when you hear His heart. That connection compels you to move, to walk in faith.

Wisdom

Wisdom is important. In fact, "wisdom is supreme—so get wisdom. And whatever else you get, get understanding" (Prov. 4:7, csb). But we need to make sure we are getting the right kind of wisdom, the right kind of counsel.

The enemy would be more than happy to give you his so-called wisdom because he knows that following his counsel will ultimately lead to your destruction, and the devil is really into destroying things. That's why the apostle James warned against the devil's kind of wisdom: "But if you have bitter envy and selfish ambition in your heart, don't boast and deny the truth. Such wisdom does not come down from above but is earthly, unspiritual, demonic. For where there is envy and selfish ambition, there is disorder and every evil practice" (Jas. 3:14–16, csb).

What you need is heavenly wisdom. Heavenly wisdom is very different from demonic wisdom. "But the wisdom from above is first pure, then peace-loving, gentle, compliant, full of mercy and good fruits, unwavering, without pretense" (Jas. 3:17, csb). Heavenly wisdom always edifies. It always builds you up and moves you toward fulfilling your destiny, your purpose in Christ. Heavenly wisdom takes head knowledge and turns it into heart transformation. It moves you into places where you are positioned for the supernatural. But if you're drinking from a different well, you're going to wind up in other places, and those places are for sure not going to be heavenly. "There is a way that seems right to a person, but its end is the way to death" (Prov. 14:12, CSB).

So how do you get wisdom? You can get wisdom through the Word of God. You can get wisdom through wise counsel. But you can also get wisdom through prayer, and that is one of the best ways to get wisdom because it is coming straight from God: "For the LORD gives wisdom; from his mouth come knowledge and understanding" (Prov. 2:6, CSB).

James 1:5–6 says, "Now if any of you lacks wisdom, he should ask God—who gives to all generously and ungrudgingly—and it will be given to him. But let him ask in faith without doubting. For the doubter is like the surging sea, driven and tossed by the wind" (CSB). I love this! If you need wisdom, all you need to do is ask. And God isn't getting out an eyedropper to give you just a tiny drop of wisdom. He gives wisdom in abundance. You can get as much wisdom as you want.

Often, we think of wisdom as something we need in order to deal with external issues we are facing, but the Holy Spirit gives us wisdom to deal with what is on the inside too. When we are taking territory for the kingdom of God in our hearts, when we are looking into the mirror of the Word of God to see what needs to be fixed, the Holy Spirit is there to provide wisdom. When we go to Him in prayer, He is there to teach us, to impart wisdom to us in the secret places of our hearts. Psalm 51:6 says, "Behold, you delight in truth in the inward being, and you teach me wisdom in the secret heart." The Lord is delighted when we come to Him, asking for wisdom to apply the truth to our hearts. And when we pray and ask for His supernatural wisdom, He will give it in abundance every time.

Pray for Your Enemies

I went to a Bible study the other day, and I asked, "How many of y'all have some enemies, people you are just so aggravated with that you really want to let them have it? How many of you ever feel like that?" Ninety percent of the people in the room raised their hands. Then I asked, "How many of y'all prayed for those people today?" One hand went up.

When you don't believe the way God believes and instead believe the way you believe, you aren't going to pray for your enemies. But when you believe the way God believes, the minute you feel someone is your enemy (whether they actually are or not), you are going to pray. And you aren't going to pray *at* the person; you are going to pray *for* the person. The more you start believing that a person is of more inherent value than your feelings, and the more you start believing that God's way is better than the way you want to do things, the more you will know you have actually accepted what God says about how you act, how you think, how you speak, how you live, and how you love. When you choose to pray for people rather than following your flesh, even though you don't know the natural outcome, there is always a supernatural reward. That is what seeking first the kingdom means. When you are in authentic relationship with Jesus, when you choose to take Him at His Word, when you choose to truly believe and act on that belief, when you seek first His kingdom, "all these things will be added to you" (Matt. 6:33).

Luke 6:38 says, "Give, and it will be given to you. Good measure, pressed down, shaken together, running over, will be put into your lap. For with the measure you use it will be measured back to you." When people read that verse, they always think about finances. And the verse definitely applies to finances, but it applies to other things too, especially if we back up and add the verse before it: "Judge not, and you will not be judged; condemn not, and you will not be condemned; forgive, and you will be forgiven; give, and it will be given to you" (vv. 37–38).

There is a lady I call Mama Vinny who goes to our church. She came up to me one day and told me about an issue she was having with someone. I asked her, "Have you prayed for them?"

Her initial reaction, just like most people's reaction when they are in the middle of being upset, was, "What?"

I said, "Well, doesn't the Bible say to pray for your enemies?" I also told Mama Vinny the verse in Luke 6 with the concept of getting back what we sow in good measure, and I asked her if she could use it in her situation.

Mama Vinny came back a week later and said, "You know, I feel a lot better."

The truth is that it is impossible to hold on to anger or a grudge against someone and pray for that person at the same time.

God says to love and pray for your enemies (Matt. 5:44). We sometimes think that praying for our enemies just means we pray for blessings rather than curses for them:

"Lord, You know I'm really upset with this person right now, so will You give her a new car?"

But if I truly understand that the kingdom of God is in me, if I truly believe that God is a God of reconciliation, if I truly choose to love my enemies, I'm going to start with the mirror: "Lord, You know I am angry. You know I'm frustrated. Please show me if I've done something wrong here. Please show me if I'm not in alignment with Your Word in this situation." Always start with the mirror first.

Let's say the person did something blatantly against the Word of God. You can still pray for that person with love, with compassion, with humility, and with a view toward reconciliation for them, not only with you but also with God. Let's say the person stole from you. You can pray, "Lord, I know that sometime in my life, I too was a thief. I know there was a thief on the cross that You forgave. Lord, I don't know why she stole from me. I don't know if she stole because of her past. I don't know if she stole because she was in dire need. Whatever the reason, Lord, I choose to forgive her, and I pray that she will have an encounter with You just like the thief on the cross did." You pray for your enemies, knowing you could have ended up caught in the same sin if it weren't for Jesus. You pray for their hearts, knowing what your heart could have been like if you had never known the Lord.

Praying for the hearts of your enemies keeps your heart pure. And you want purity of heart, for the Word says, "Blessed are the pure in heart, for they shall see God" (Matt. 5:8). You also want a pure heart because, again, you speak about what your heart is full of: "Out of the abundance of the heart his mouth speaks" (Luke 6:45).

The prayer that's coming out of your mouth is realigning what's right and what's true.

Guard Your Heart

When you begin to pray with a pure heart, when your prayer realigns you with what is good and right and true, it guards your heart from harboring any bitterness. Otherwise, your heart would be hardened because you would be counseled by the enemy. That's why taking thoughts captive is important. That's why putting the Word of God out in the atmosphere is important. You're guarding your heart because you're not allowing in anything that'll harden your heart. You're basically filling your heart with the Word like it's rivers of living water. You are being cleansed by the washing of the water of the Word.

In Scripture the heart is far more than a mere organ; it represents the inner self—where thoughts, emotions, desires, and decisions are formed. The heart is also the source of relationships. The Bible makes it clear that in our relationships our ability to love, forgive, and care for one another springs from what is in the heart.

Your heart is like a control center. Imagine a modern airplane's cockpit. Just as every flight decision comes from the cockpit, our actions and decisions originate in our hearts. A well-functioning cockpit ensures a safe flight, while a faulty one can lead to disaster. A well-functioning heart leads to abundant life.

The well-functioning heart starts with loving God: "You shall love the Lord your God with all your heart and with all your soul and with all your might" (Deut. 6:5). If that isn't in place, nothing else will be.

Proverbs 4:23 says, "Above all else, guard your heart, for everything you do flows from it" (NIV). The heart is the wellspring of life, influencing our decisions and actions. Neglecting its care invites harmful influences that can damage our relationships—including our relationship with Jesus.

Imagine your heart as a castle. Without strong walls and vigilant guards, invaders (negative influences such as anger, bitterness, fear, or sin) can easily breach the defenses and cause havoc. Guarding your heart means regularly reinforcing its defenses—through prayer, Scripture, and accountability—to keep it secure from spiritual attacks.

Even though castle walls are often made of stone, that is the last thing you want your heart to be like. Even though you need to guard your heart and you want your heart to have strong defenses, you don't want your heart to be hard. Hardness of heart is never good. Pharaoh hardened his heart, and it led to his ultimate destruction—but not before he saw the land he ruled ravaged by plagues, one of which claimed the life of his firstborn son. Proverbs 28:14 says, "Whoever hardens his heart will fall into calamity." Hardness of heart grieves the Lord (Mark 3:5).

But there is good news. Remember that the Lord promised to give us new hearts: "I will give you a new heart and put a new spirit within you; I will remove your heart of stone and give you a heart of flesh" (Ezek. 36:26, CSB). The heart of stone symbolizes stubbornness, rebellion, and insensitivity, while the heart of flesh represents openness, responsiveness, and compassion.

When you guard your heart through prayer, it makes you sensitive to the promptings of the Holy Spirit. A soft heart is humble and open to receiving the Word of the

Lord. Humility is the first step toward change. A humble heart allows you to pray, "Create in me a clean heart, O God, and renew a right spirit within me" (Ps. 51:10).

A heart of flesh allows you to walk by faith. A heart of flesh is a place where the peace of God can rule. A heart of flesh can be refreshed in the presence of the Lord. When you have a heart that is responsive to the Holy Spirit, in times of trouble, trial, or testing, the Spirit will move you and guide you into the truth.

Prayer guards our hearts, but it also renews our hearts. A renewed heart is sensitive to the heart of God. It guides us to live in a way that mirrors God's compassion and mercy. Remember, "out of the abundance of the heart his mouth speaks" (Luke 6:45). A good person produces good out of the good that is stored up in their heart. You want a heart that is full of the love of God, full of the Word of God, and full of the Spirit of God.

How to Pray

Sometimes our problem is we don't know how to pray. We pray like God is a Mexican piñata or a genie granting wishes. We have a wish list we expect God to fulfill, but we ask for things that are not in the will of God. But prayer is an exchange. It is a sharing between heaven and earth. Prayer builds the kingdom of God inside you, in your heart, so when we all get together, you bring the presence of God's kingdom with you. We need to learn to just spend time with the Lord and have that exchange between heaven and earth.

Prayer is a heart-to-heart conversation. I want you to imagine sitting down for a deep, thoughtful, honest conversation with a trusted friend. God wants you to spend

The Power of Prayer

time with Him in prayer that is just like that kind of conversation. He wants you to share your heart with Him, and He wants to share His heart with you.

I was reading John 15 the other day and meditating on it. It's a passage I have read a lot, but it hit me differently this time. That's one of the things I love about the Word of God. It is living and active, so you never know how it's going to hit your heart.

So John 15 starts out with Jesus saying He is the vine. He talked about remaining in Him, being pruned, and producing fruit, and He said the Father is glorified when we produce fruit (vv. 1–2, 8). Then Jesus talked about what it means to be a friend: "No one has greater love than this: to lay down his life for his friends" (v. 13, CSB). That's deep. That's powerful. But the part that got me is verse 15: "I have called you friends, because I have made known to you everything I have heard from my Father" (CSB).

Did you catch that?

Jesus is clearly your friend because He laid down His life for you. But when He calls you His friend is when He gets to talk to you, to tell you everything the Father has told Him. Jesus was saying, "I want to tell you everything because you're My friend."

Jesus considers me His friend? That makes me want to pray, "I want You to tell me everything, Lord! I want to know it all!"

That's the heart of prayer. That's where it starts. Prayer is a conversation with almighty God, the Creator of the universe, the Alpha and Omega, the Redeemer, the commander of the army of the Lord, the Ancient of Days, the everlasting Father, the Holy One of Israel, the King of kings and Lord of lords, the righteous judge—who also happens to be your friend.

When the disciples asked Jesus to teach them to pray, He taught them a model prayer. We call it the Lord's Prayer. The prayer starts, "Our Father in heaven, your name be honored as holy" (Matt. 6:9, CSB). When you come to the Father, He's our Father because He's not just your Father; he's my Father too. I know I like all my kids to get along with one other, and that's how our Father is too.

When you come to our Father in prayer, you are showing Him the reverence due His name. You are showing Him honor. You don't just come to Him any kind of way. On the streets we used to say, "You put some respect on my name." Well, you need to come to God the same way because He is our Father. You have to put some respect on His name.

"Your kingdom come" (Matt. 6:10, CSB). Prayer is an exchange between heaven and earth. It's not just us asking for things from a selfish place. It's the exchange that brings the kingdom of heaven down to earth. And since the kingdom of God is in you, when you pray, "Your kingdom come," it's about the kingdom of God advancing in your own heart.

When I was studying the Lord's Prayer, I noticed there is a period after "Your kingdom come." I was used to going right from "Your kingdom come" to "Your will be done." When I noticed that period, I got more excited over a punctuation mark than I ever had before in my life!

The period means you come to a full stop. The period means that "kingdom come" and "will be done" aren't simultaneous events. It's saying that "kingdom come" happens first, and then "will be done." The will is not done unless the kingdom has come. That period, that stop, means His kingdom rules and reigns. When God's kingdom comes, it governs your life. When God's kingdom comes and is inside you, you are choosing to be ruled by the King of that kingdom—and He is the King of kings. You are saying, "King Jesus, You reign; You have authority over my life. You have authority over my decisions. Your kingdom has come, so Your will will be done in my life, on earth as it is heaven."

"Your kingdom come" is a supernatural imparting of the kingdom of God to you, and it results in the supernatural will of God happening in your life. Heaven will be coming out of you because you are being led by the Spirit. You are walking in faith according to what God is saying. You are allowing the living Word to rule and reign in your heart, and this will allow the supernatural to not only work in you but also spill over to others through you.

"Your will be done on earth as it is in heaven" means it starts in me (Matt. 6:10, CSB). It starts in you. The kingdom of God is in us. Our hearts are the first place the kingdom of God takes territory on the earth. It doesn't start on the outside with physical territory. It starts on the inside.

If you don't have the kingdom of God taking territory on the earth inside your heart, if you don't have that happening inside, then you have selfish ambition, which the Bible says is demonic.

There sometimes comes a point when everything on the outside looks fine. You're doing good things. You're doing all the right things. You're not doing the things the old you used to do. Your friends are in Christ. But if the kingdom of God isn't taking territory inside your heart, there is a problem. Because here's the thing: If the enemy can get you to take something good and misprioritize it, it becomes an idol. It takes up space in your heart that should be taken by the kingdom. When that happens, your focus is doing good things rather than doing the will of God.

Let me say that another way. "Your will be done on earth as it is in heaven" means you do the will of God instead of the good things. Don't get me wrong—the will of God is good because God is good. But just because something is good does not mean that it is the will of God for you to do it. It is an easy trap to fall into because we tend to get into comparison mode. We look at someone doing something good to build the kingdom and think, "I should do that too." But the thing is, God's will for that person and His purpose for that person are not the same as they are for you. Yes, we all have this, like, overarching purpose to glorify God, but God has different plans and purposes for each of us.

Don't fall for the messed-up thinking that says you're doing things for God when you are really just doing good things to please yourself. Jesus said,

> Not everyone who says to me, "Lord, Lord," will enter the kingdom of heaven, but only *the one who does the will of my Father* in heaven. On that day many will say to me, "Lord, Lord, didn't we prophesy in your name, drive out demons in your name, and do many miracles in your name?" Then I will announce to them, "I never knew you."
> —Matthew 7:21–23, csb, emphasis added

Do His will, not yours.

"Give us today our daily bread" (Matt. 6:11, csb). Jesus

is the Bread of Life (John 6:48). When you pray, "Give us today our daily bread," you're asking Jesus to give you what you need today. You are saying, "Give me the bread. Give me the Word. Give me You. Give me revelation. Give me everything of You that I need for today." You need Jesus. You need the Word. You need revelation, for "without revelation people run wild" (Prov. 29:18, CSB).

Notice that nowhere in this prayer did Jesus say, "Present your wish list to God." He didn't say to tell God everything you want. The proper perspective about prayer is never about what you want. It's about relationship with God. It's about having the perspective that God's kingdom rules and reigns. So you are asking for the things you need in order to accomplish the things that are in the will of God for you to accomplish. Remember, God already knows what you need. "But seek first the kingdom of God and his righteousness, and all these things will be provided for you" (Matt. 6:33, CSB).

"Forgive us our debts, as we also have forgiven our debtors" (Matt. 6:12, CSB). Remember, Jesus said, "Whenever you pray..." (Matt. 6:5, CSB). That means when you come to God in prayer and say, "Forgive us our debts, as we also have forgiven our debtors," you should have already forgiven your debtors. Unforgiveness is bad news. Jesus said, "For if you forgive others their offenses, your heavenly Father will forgive you as well. But if you don't forgive others, your Father will not forgive your offenses" (Matt. 6:14–15, CSB).

A kingdom-of-God heart has no room for unforgiveness. It has no room for bitterness. It has no room for grudges. It has no room for hardness of heart. If you have those things in your heart, it is time to look into the mirror of the Word. It is time for the washing of the water of the Word. It is time to let God cleanse you of all unrighteousness. It is time for a little supernatural heart surgery.

"And do not bring us into temptation, but deliver us from the evil one" (Matt. 6:13, CSB). When we are in an authentic relationship with Jesus, when our hearts are governed by the King of kings, this part of the prayer means we know where our strength comes from—and it isn't from us. It means that we should never desire tests, trials, and temptations just so we can have a dramatic story to tell. It means that we know we have been forgiven of our sins, but we don't want to return to them again. We don't want to fall for the enemy's traps and schemes and lies. We want hearts where Jesus rules and reigns.

So when we pray, it's about aligning our hearts with heaven. It's about aligning ourselves with the will and the Word of God so we can receive power from the Holy Spirit to live beyond our natural limitations. Prayer is about an exchange between heaven and earth that will allow us to walk by faith and to live supernaturally.

Chapter 8
THE HELP OF THE HOLY SPIRIT

THE SPIRIT OF Jesus doesn't lead you into just anything. He leads you into truth. If I'm in one place and Jesus wants me somewhere else, the Spirit will tug me the way Jesus wants me to go. It's always going to move me into His character, into His nature, into something that lines up with His Word. The Holy Spirit doesn't move you aimlessly. He always moves you into truth.

We need the help of the Holy Spirit. The Holy Spirit is a gift Jesus asked the Father to give us: "And I will ask the Father, and He will give you another Comforter (Counselor, Helper, Intercessor, Advocate, Strengthener, and Standby), that He may remain with you forever" (John 14:16, AMPC). As we chase Jesus, as we develop authentic relationship with the Lord, the Holy Spirit moves in our hearts and in our lives. As we walk by faith and build the kingdom, He is always there to help, to comfort, to counsel, to strengthen, and to intercede. And it may seem crazy that the Holy Spirit fills all those roles and more in your life, but it isn't crazy—it's God.

God Isn't a Piñata

As believers we need to be sensitive to the leading of the Holy Spirit. I think one of the areas where we become hard of hearing and struggle to follow the Spirit's lead is with our finances.

As I've said before, sometimes we view God like a piñata. We treat Him like a genie in a lamp, or even like a vending machine. We sometimes get this mentality that if we put $1,000 in the offering plate today, God will give us $10,000 tomorrow. That's not how God works.

Did God say, "Bring the full tenth into the storehouse so that there may be food in my house. Test me in this way....See if I will not open the floodgates of heaven and pour out a blessing for you without measure" (Mal. 3:10, CSB)? Absolutely. Again, did Jesus say, "Give, and it will be given to you; a good measure—pressed down, shaken together, and running over—will be poured into your lap. For with the measure you use, it will be measured back to you" (Luke 6:38, CSB)? Definitely. That means it is 100 percent possible that God will give you $10,000 if you give Him $1,000.

But let's consider the whole counsel of God. Jesus, talking about money and wealth, also said, "Whoever is faithful in very little is also faithful in much, and whoever is unrighteous in very little is also unrighteous in much" (Luke 16:10, CSB). If you're making a decent salary but you're up to your eyeballs in credit card debt, you're not tithing, and you're more concerned with your reputation and possessions than you are with building the kingdom, why in the world would God want to supernaturally give you an extra $9,000? You're not making wise financial choices, so why would God want to give you more money to waste?

Think about it like this: If you went up to a soda machine and it had a sign that said, "Out of Order," would you put your money in it? No, of course you wouldn't. So why would God continue to give you things when you're out of order?

This is a mirror moment. The Word of God says, "No servant can serve two masters, since either he will hate one and love the other, or he will be devoted to one and despise the other. You cannot serve both God and money" (Luke 16:13, csb). When you look into the mirror of the Word of God, do you see something in you that needs to be fixed? Do you need to get the way you handle your finances aligned with the Word, the will, and the heart of God? If the Holy Spirit is leading you to do something, you need to do it.

FRUIT OF THE SPIRIT

When you are not living according to the Word of God, you end up with all this loopiness in your life. When you are doing whatever you want, you are not going to bear fruit. But when you are submitted to the authority of the Word of God and are being led by the Spirit, fruit is produced in your life. The Bible says a lot about the fruit in the life of a believer. When the religious leaders—whom the Bible refers to as, among other things, "brood of vipers," "hypocrites," and "whitewashed tombs"—went out to the Jordan River to be baptized by John the Baptist, John told them to "bear fruit in keeping with repentance" (Matt. 3:7–8; 23:27). Jesus taught, "You'll recognize them by their fruit. Are grapes gathered from thornbushes or figs from thistles? In the same way, every good tree produces good fruit, but a bad tree produces bad fruit. A good tree can't produce bad fruit; neither can a bad tree produce good fruit" (Matt. 7:16–18, CSB). And again, He also said, "But he who received seed on the good ground is he who hears the word and understands it, who indeed bears fruit and produces: some a hundredfold, some sixty, some thirty" (Matt. 13:23, NKJV).

The world will recognize the kingdom of God in us when we bear good fruit. The world will see the supernatural at work in us when our good fruit production is exponential. But we can't bear good fruit without being in a heart-level relationship with the Lord:

> I am the true vine, and my Father is the vinedresser. Every branch in me that does not bear fruit he takes away, and every branch that does bear fruit he prunes, that it may bear more fruit....Abide in me, and I in you. As the branch cannot bear fruit by itself, unless it abides in the vine, neither can you, unless you abide in me. I am the vine; you are the branches. Whoever abides in me and I in him, he it is that bears much fruit, for apart from me you can do nothing.
>
> —John 15:1–2, 4–5

The key to bearing good fruit is relationship—Jesus abiding in you, and you abiding in Him. *Abide* is one of those words we don't use very often these days, and when it is used, it often means to tolerate or accept. But that is not what the word means in this passage. Instead, it means to stay. The Greek word for *abide* means to stay, to continue, to dwell, to be held, to continue being present, and to remain.[1] Good fruit is the result of continued connection with God. It is the result of holding on to Him while He holds on to you. It is the result of God living in you and of understanding that "it is no longer I who live, but Christ who lives in me. And the life I now live in the flesh I live by faith in the Son of God, who loved me and gave himself for me" (Gal. 2:20).

So what is good fruit? What does good fruit look like? The Bible gives us the answer. Good fruit is the fruit of the Spirit: "But the fruit of the Spirit is love, joy, peace, patience, kindness, goodness, faithfulness, gentleness, self-control" (Gal. 5:22–23).

Sometimes I hear people say things like, "I can never have self-control." That's not true. In fact, it's a lie from the enemy. If you are being led by the Spirit, then you have the fruit of the Spirit being produced in your life. So when a believer with a history of lack of self-control all of a sudden is demonstrating self-control, it isn't, "Wow! He really learned to control himself." Instead, it's, "Wow! He made Jesus Lord in his life and is being led by the Spirit. Look at the fruit!"

And a key thing to remember about the fruit of the Spirit is that it's the *fruit*, not the *fruits*. God doesn't pick and choose, as if there's a bowl of fruit and He's going to pick the apple and the orange but leave the banana and the pear. It's not like that. When you have the Holy Spirit abiding in you, you get the fruit, and you get it all. The Holy Spirit supernaturally produces the fruit of righteousness and transforms the believer into the image of Christ.

Another key thing to remember about fruit is that it is designed to be eaten. I grew up in Puerto Rico, so we had a lot of plastic fruit in the house. It wasn't edible. But fruit is supposed to be eaten. The reason we have the fruit of the Spirit is not for us. It's for building the kingdom. When someone interacting with you gets a bite of that patience in a situation where impatience and anger is expected, it's going to make them wonder, "How can he be so patient?" In a world that is becoming more and more unkind, when they taste kindness in you, it is going to get their attention. "Why is she being kind? I don't deserve her kindness." The fruit of the Spirit is part of the process of transforming you into the image of Christ, from glory to glory. When people see the fruit of the Spirit in you, they are seeing Jesus. You are enabling them to "taste and see that the LORD is good!" (Ps. 34:8). God gives you this beautiful fruit so someone else can see it and want it for themselves.

The fruit of the Spirit is like Evangelism 101. You know the saying, "You can lead a horse to water, but you can't make him drink"? My response to that is, "True, but you can sure make him thirsty." We can't force people to come to Jesus. We can't force them to repent and make Jesus their Lord and Savior. We can't make them get saved so they can live abundant lives of freedom. But we can make them want it. We can make them hungry for what we have. We can make them hungry for the peace that passes all understanding. We can make them hungry for unspeakable joy. We can make them hungry for the goodness of God. We can make them hungry for the supernatural.

When we are walking by faith and bearing good fruit, we are just setting the table for people to eat. The Holy Spirit will do the rest.

LEAN ON THE LORD, NOT YOUR GIFTS

I want the world to know Jesus so we can all experience the supernatural—the signs and wonders that follow a person who is walking by faith in authentic relationship with the Lord. But when I look at the church these days, it often looks like we are doing it backward. It's as if 1 Corinthians 12, which discusses the supernatural gifts given to the body of Christ, was written just for us.

The church in Corinth had been arguing about gifts. There were believers who thought they were more important than others or deserved more honor because of the gifts they had. There were people being prideful about their gifts, as if they were the source of the gift rather than the Holy Spirit. It was causing discord and disunity.

That's where we are at. The church is arguing about the gifts. We are putting the gifts and the people who have them up on a pedestal, not realizing how many people are leaning on their gifts rather than on the Lord. We are so mesmerized by the gifts that we aren't bothering to look to see if there is fruit. Everybody's looking at a guy who may not make it into heaven, but he sure can operate in the gifts. The gifts of God are irrevocable (Rom. 11:29), so God doesn't take away gifts just because they are being misused. As we've mentioned, 1 Corinthians 13:1–3 says,

> If I speak in the tongues of men and of angels, but have not love, I am a noisy gong or a clanging cymbal. And if I have prophetic powers, and understand all mysteries and all knowledge, and if I have all faith, so as to remove mountains, but have not love, I am nothing. If I give away all I have, and if I

deliver up my body to be burned, but have not love,
I gain nothing.

When we operate in the gifts of the Spirit, we are supposed to be operating in love. The apostle Paul went on to tell the church at Corinth what love looks like:

> Love is patient and kind; love does not envy or boast; it is not arrogant or rude. It does not insist on its own way; it is not irritable or resentful; it does not rejoice at wrongdoing, but rejoices with the truth. Love bears all things, believes all things, hopes all things, endures all things.
> —1 Corinthians 13:4–7

When are you are being led by the Spirit, you are being led by love, for "God is love" (1 John 4:8). However, so many of us aren't being led by love because we have a superiority complex. It's almost as if we think we're Jesus. But no matter how many spiritual gifts you have, no matter how many times you have been a vessel of the supernatural, you aren't Jesus. You can't save anyone. You can't heal anyone. You can't set anyone free. That's God's part. When you start thinking you're Jesus and you lean on your gifts, you don't have to live through Jesus and for Jesus. But that is a dangerous road. God's gifts are irrevocable, but you don't want to get to heaven and hear, "Depart from Me…"

Our attitude with regard to our gifts needs to be one of humility. Remember, when you are operating in pride, you are being counseled by the enemy. When you operate in humility, you are being counseled by the Holy Spirit. Your attitude about your gifts should be, "I'm totally dependent on You, Holy Spirit, because I don't know how to do this."

Here's what I've learned. I'm a mere man. I know what I can do. I know what seemed right to me, but when I did what seemed right to me instead of chasing after Jesus and His ways, it always led me to destruction. You know what I can do? I can destroy everything. I can ruin everything. And that's what happens when we lean on our own understanding, when we lean on our gifts, when we lean on ourselves. My total dependency has to be on the leading of the Holy Spirit. My dependency has to be on my relationship with Jesus Christ.

One of the issues with the way we idolize spiritual gifts is we have that skewed perspective of the supernatural. We see someone get out of a wheelchair, and we think the person with the gift of healing must have this amazing relationship with the Lord. But that isn't always the case. What happens when we look for other evidence of the supernatural operating in that person's life? What happens if we look for good fruit? Good fruit is supernatural. If we look for that fruit, are we going to find it? Are we going to see love, joy, peace, patience, faithfulness, kindness, goodness, gentleness, and self-control? Or are we going to see the works of the flesh, like sexual immorality, jealousy, fits of anger, division, rivalries, and envy? (See Galatians 5:19–23.)

When we don't look at the fruit of the Spirit as supernatural, it's easy to focus on the gift rather than the gift giver. With the way our human tendencies are, if we see a movie on deliverance and everybody's talking about deliverance, then everybody wants to be a deliverance minister tomorrow. Yet you don't read the Word, you don't pray, you don't fast, you don't renew your mind, and you don't understand the gospel internally. In other words, you don't know how to die daily. It's still about you. You're still full of pride, and yet you want to go lead people. But before Jesus sent the disciples out to deliver people, He had them get to know Him first. Your ministry, your calling, your purpose, and your gifts are all supposed to come out of relationship—out of a deep, intimate, authentic, heart-level relationship with Jesus.

Look at social media. If the apostle James were around, he would say, "You have to be quick to listen and slow to type." You may want to be a deliverance minister, but have you allowed the Holy Spirit to take territory for the kingdom of God in your heart? Does your character line up with how the Word describes a deliverance minister?

> And the Lord's servant must not be quarrelsome but kind to everyone, able to teach, patiently enduring evil, correcting his opponents with gentleness. God may perhaps grant them repentance leading to a knowledge of the truth, and they may come to their senses and escape from the snare of the devil, after being captured by him to do his will.
> —2 Timothy 2:24–26

As servants of the Lord, if we want to see deliverance, we are called to be kind, patient, gentle, and not quarrelsome. That's not happening very often these days.

Everybody jumps on social media like a bunch of chickens chasing corn. All these influencers are saying, "Oh, I'm doing this for the Lord." Well, the Lord separates the sheep from the goats. I feel like so many influencers who are supposedly all about Jesus aren't chasing Jesus at all. Some of them aren't even chasing miracles. They're chasing clicks. They're chasing likes. They're chasing followers. Let me speak the truth in love: If you are more focused on people following you than following Jesus, your heart is in the wrong place.

Sometimes I look at all these influencers and think, "Where's the compassion? Where's the empathy? Where's the kindness? Where's the self-control? Where's the truth? Where's having the heart of a servant?" This whole internet thing draws us away from the Lord all day long.

If you want to truly experience the supernatural, you need to be chasing Jesus, not chasing miracles or followers. You need to be leaning on the Spirit, not on the gift He has given you. You need to be developing that close friendship with Jesus rather than putting on a show. Good fruit only comes when you abide in the vine.

THE FLESH FALLS

One day, my wife and I floated around a lazy river at a resort for several hours. I didn't put on any sunscreen before we went out. Big mistake. I'm a white Puerto Rican, and I got sunburned so bad. The pain was horrible. My skin was on fire. When I looked in the mirror the next day, it wasn't good. My skin was so red, and I was thinking, "This hurts so much!" Then I noticed that my skin was peeling off in some areas. That was when the Lord spoke to me. He said, "When you spend time in the Son, the flesh falls."

Boom! Revelation.

If you have ever had a sunburn, you know that when you spend time in the sun, your flesh ends up falling off, that outer layer of skin that got burned. But when you spend time with Jesus, the Son of God, your flesh falls too.

We've talked about how God is a refining fire. And we know that fire doesn't feel good. But it's good pain. It's like the pain when you work out. It hurts at the time, but it is making you stronger and moving you toward your goal. The refining fire causes your flesh to fall. And when your flesh falls, you are getting stronger. You are becoming more like Jesus.

But let's be honest. We avoid taking up our crosses to follow Jesus because we don't want anything that may cause pain. We sometimes just want to say, "No, thanks. I'm good." But when we do that, we will miss out on the supernatural.

You might say the gospel is upside-down or backward. You might even say the gospel is crazy. That's because in the gospel suffering builds you up—as long as you are moving in the same direction as the Holy Spirit. When you are in an intimate relationship with God, He is constantly washing you with His Word. He is changing you. He is transforming you. That's why we need the Holy Spirit. He puts the Word deep into our hearts and strengthens us so we can overcome the enemy, so we can overcome sin. You can't overcome sin in your own strength. Sanctification empowers believers to overcome. You overcome when you surrender.

Romans 6:11 says, "So you also must consider yourselves dead to sin and alive to God in Christ Jesus." You are dead to sin and alive to God. That means every time you say no to sin, you're saying yes to a promise. A no to the flesh is a yes to heaven. When you die to your sin, you're alive to God.

As we mature as followers of Jesus, we are led by the Spirit to "put to death the deeds of the body" (Rom. 8:13). God has called us to be His children. He did not give us a spirit of slavery so we would keep falling back into the bondage of sin. He gave us the Spirit of adoption to testify that we are His children. And because we are His children, we have His Spirit to lead us—if we choose to follow Him.

I had this revelation one day. I was upset with my wife, and when I said something about it, everything went sideways. When I went to talk to the Lord about it, the first thing He said was, "Wow."

"Why do You say that, Lord?" I asked.

"I'm going to ask you a question."

"What's that?"

"Do you believe Ruthy has Jesus in her life? Do you believe I live in her?"

"Yeah."

"You would talk to Me like that?"

Ouch.

That was conviction, and that is how the Holy Spirit works.

The Holy Spirit helps us with sanctification. He is Jehovah Qadash, "the Lord who sanctifies you" (Lev. 20:8). *Sanctify* means to consecrate, to set apart, to make holy, to separate, to be clean.[2] When the Holy Spirit sanctifies you, He is setting you apart for the Lord. He is consecrating you for the divine purposes of your life. He is making your flesh fall. He is cleaning you up and making you holy. Sanctification makes us more like Jesus. And do you know what the Holy Spirit uses to sanctify you? The Word of God. When Jesus was in the Garden of Gethsemane before He was crucified, He prayed, "Sanctify them by the truth; your word is truth" (John 17:17, CSB). Again, Ephesians 5:25–27 says,

> Christ loved the church and gave himself up for her, that he might sanctify her, having cleansed her by the washing of water with the word, so that he might present the church to himself in splendor,

without spot or wrinkle or any such thing, that she might be holy and without blemish.

The Holy Spirit also helps us with transformation. He transforms our minds and transforms our character to make us more like Jesus. Everything Christlike is produced by the Spirit of God. It's about being made in His image, being changed from glory to glory: "But we all, with unveiled face, beholding as in a mirror the glory of the Lord, are being transformed into the same image from glory to glory, just as by the Spirit of the Lord" (2 Cor. 3:18, NKJV).

The only One who can transform your heart is the Holy Spirit. When He does that, you can actually discern what the will of God is. It provides believers with supernatural discernment to recognize true and false spirits, teachings, and prophetic revelations:

> Beloved, do not believe every spirit, but test the spirits to see whether they are from God, for many false prophets have gone out into the world. By this you know the Spirit of God: every spirit that confesses that Jesus Christ has come in the flesh is from God, and every spirit that does not confess Jesus is not from God. This is the spirit of the antichrist, which you heard was coming and now is in the world already. Little children, you are from God and have overcome them, for he who is in you is greater than he who is in the world.
> —1 JOHN 4:1–4

If you want authenticity, you need the Holy Spirit. You want something that's real; you don't want the fake thing.

The Holy Spirit testifies to what's real and authentic so we don't miss it.

The Holy Spirit is also the source of intimacy with God. The Spirit fosters deep communion between believers and God. He enables you to have experiential knowledge of the supernatural presence of the Lord.

But if you want to experience all these things of the Spirit, you have to come to the end of yourself. You have to let your flesh fall. If you don't, you'll never tap into everything the Holy Spirit has for you—you'll never tap into God's deeper purpose for your life.

Revelation

Revelation is important. The ability to understand the will of God and the way He is moving and working in the world enables us to see the supernatural. Revelation also helps keep us on the right track, walking the way we are supposed to go. Proverbs 29:18 says, "Without revelation people run wild, but one who follows divine instruction will be happy" (CSB).

The Holy Spirit illuminates the Scripture. The Holy Spirit gives us revelation. In other words, He reveals spiritual truth. He brings understanding. He unveils divine mysteries. Spiritual realities cannot be discerned through the natural eye or with the natural mind.

The Holy Spirit is always our source of revelation. The Word of God says,

> But as it is written: "Eye has not seen, nor ear heard, nor have entered into the heart of man the things which God has prepared for those who love Him." But *God has revealed them to us through His Spirit.*

> For the Spirit searches all things, yes, the deep things of God. For what man knows the things of a man except the spirit of the man which is in him? Even so no one knows the things of God except the Spirit of God. Now we have received, not the spirit of the world, but the Spirit who is from God, that we might know the things that have been freely given to us by God.
>
> These things we also speak, not in words which man's wisdom teaches but which the Holy Spirit teaches, comparing spiritual things with spiritual. But the natural man does not receive the things of the Spirit of God, for they are foolishness to him; nor can he know them, because they are spiritually discerned.
>
> —1 CORINTHIANS 2:9–14, NKJV, EMPHASIS ADDED

For you to understand the deep things of God, they must be revealed to you by the Holy Spirit. And without divine revelation we run wild. The Hebrew word translated "run wild" in Proverbs 29:18 means to show a lack of restraint, to let go unbridled, to loosen, to expose, and to perish.[3] When we don't have divine revelation, we lack direction. We lack guidance. Lack of restraint may seem like freedom, but that is a lie from the enemy. Proverbs 25:28 says, "Whoever has no rule over his own spirit is like a city broken down, without walls" (NKJV). When we run wild, we are exposed to the fiery darts of the enemy, and his plan is to steal, kill, and destroy.

Divine revelation is like a prophetic word straight from God. When the Holy Spirit provides deeper insight into God's Word, it's like a rhema word just for you.

When Jesus was born, there was a man named Simeon

The Help of the Holy Spirit

living in Jerusalem, "waiting for the Consolation of Israel, and the Holy Spirit was upon him. And it had been revealed to him by the Holy Spirit that he would not see death before he had seen the Lord's Christ" (Luke 2:25-26, NKJV). Simeon knew the Messiah's first coming was going to be during his lifetime, and he recognized Jesus—again, because of the revelation of the Spirit—when Joseph and Mary brought Him to the temple. Simeon took the baby Jesus in his arms and blessed the Lord. He also prophesied about Jesus. The last thing Simeon said was that through Jesus "the thoughts of many hearts may be revealed" (Luke 2:35, NKJV).

You see, the Holy Spirit doesn't just reveal the things of God to us. He reveals things about ourselves. He shows us what is in our hearts, even the things we have buried way down deep. And that's God. He doesn't want you carrying around wounds and burdens and guilt and shame and condemnation like a bunch of heavy baggage. He doesn't reveal what is in your heart because He wants to make you feel bad. He reveals what is in your heart so He can heal you. He is "the LORD who heals you" (Exod. 15:26, CSB). He reveals to heal. Jesus confirmed this when He read the prophecy about Himself from the Book of Isaiah in the synagogue in Nazareth:

> The Spirit of the LORD is upon Me, because He has anointed Me to preach the gospel to the poor; He has sent Me to heal the brokenhearted, to proclaim liberty to the captives and recovery of sight to the blind, to set at liberty those who are oppressed; to proclaim the acceptable year of the LORD.
> —LUKE 4:18-19, NKJV

The Holy Spirit is the bondage breaker. The Holy Spirit is the One who frees you from oppression. He removes limitations. He empowers you for ministry. He is the agent of healings and miracles. When you have divine revelation from the Holy Spirit, when you are led by the Spirit, you can operate in the power and authority of Jesus Christ, living by faith and advancing the kingdom of God.

Chapter 9
LIVING A LIFE OF EXPECTATION

HAVE YOU EVER wondered why some people seem to experience the miraculous consistently, while others feel as though their lives are ordinary? The key isn't in a special anointing reserved for the exclusivity of pastors, missionaries, and spiritual leaders. Rather, it lies in something beautifully simple. And I like using the word *simple* because I feel like the gospel is simple, and I think a lot of times we overcomplicate things that are simple. So the key to experiencing the miraculous is beautifully simple, yet profoundly powerful—it is living expectantly.

Living expectantly means waking up every day and anticipating that God will actively and intimately intervene in your everyday life. It means opening your eyes and having the ability to see God's fingerprints on every situation, whether it's big or small. Living expectantly means having a heart that's prepared to respond when the Holy Spirit nudges you toward the extraordinary, toward the miraculous, toward the supernatural.

When I got out of prison, I attended a school called All Nations. Every day when we got to class, I had a testimony. There were days that if I hadn't gotten up, nobody would have shared a testimony. But since I had a testimony every day, I guess it got old at a certain point. So the teacher told me to shorten my testimonies. I learned from that—I'm a talker, and I can be wordy, so being told to shorten my testimonies was fine.

But I still had a testimony every day. I was in class with all these young people, and it seemed as if they only had testimonies here or there. They wondered why I always had a testimony, so I said, "I have testimonies because I put myself in the situations to actually have a testimony." It wasn't that I had a special anointing or a special gift. I just had an expectation that God was going to move when I stepped out in faith.

For example, we would go to Breckenridge, Texas, where they sold a lot of dope and all the kinds of stuff I did in my past. When you were going somewhere in the car with me, I had rules. Whenever we stopped, if you were the reason we stopped, you had to go talk to somebody about Jesus. So if you got in the car with me and we stopped because you needed a bathroom break, you had to talk to somebody before you got back in the car. If we stopped because you were hungry, you had to talk to someone. When someone new got in my car, the others would warn them, "Oh man, Juan is going to make you talk to somebody."

I saw so many crazy things doing that. Well, they weren't actually crazy—they were God. One time we stopped at the gas station. When we got out, we saw a trailer there. Everyone in the car felt like the Lord was telling us to go talk to the people in the trailer. One of the girls said, "I feel like somebody in their family has cancer." So we went to go talk to them. We said, "Hey, can we pray for you?"

At first they were kind of offended. The guy was kind

of cranky, and he said, "I don't need no prayer. Talk to my sister."

His sister came out and was kind of cranky. She said, "What are you guys gonna pray? We're Catholic." Being Catholic has nothing to do with praying, but it's funny how people think. Then she said, "We're just on our way to see my sister who has cancer."

We were tripping out when she said that since that is what God had told one of the girls in the car with us. God used a carload of students at a gas station in the middle of Texas to do the supernatural—not because they were extra special or super gifted but because they were led by the Spirit and expected God to move.

Miracles aren't reserved for special occasions. They are God's love language. He is constantly speaking affection, power, and presence into our daily routines when we choose to live expectant lives. The Lord delights in you. He loves it when you become attuned to the gentle whispers of His declarations on the earth. He loves it when you hear His voice and follow Him. So why wouldn't He get involved at the gas station or anywhere else? God can move anywhere at any time and in any way. We just need to follow His lead.

Another time, I was spending the afternoon at the mall. I got a simple impression from the Holy Spirit that prompted me to speak encouragement into the life of a complete stranger. That actually happens to me all the time because I talk to people all the time. I admit there are times when I get a little lazy, but most of the time I'm going to have a conversation with whomever God puts in my path. I will ask them their name and maybe another question, and if I feel the nudge from the Holy Spirit, I will begin to talk about whatever the Holy Spirit puts on my heart. When I first started doing that, there were times I hesitated. Doubt would start to creep in. But even when I was wrestling with doubt, I would choose to step out in faith because I wanted to be obedient to what God was telling me to do. If you're moving by sight, the doubt will win. That's why you need to walk by faith. That's your part. And when you do your part, God will do His.

So I was at the mall, and I started speaking encouragement to a woman, a total stranger. Then tears started filling her eyes. She told me that she had prayed that morning for a sign from God. I can't tell you how many times things like that have happened. I didn't know what was going on in this lady's life or in her heart. I didn't know why God wanted me to speak encouragement to her. I just believed God when He told me what to do, and I stepped out in faith. And for her that moment was a clear miracle. It was supernatural. It was God. She didn't have to get out of a wheelchair. The Creator of the universe cared enough about her and her struggles to have a complete stranger speak the exact words of encouragement she needed to hear. And beyond the words, God showed her that He sees her, He loves her, He hears her prayers, and He answers.

When we recognize the supernatural at work in our lives and in the lives of others, it builds our faith. That faith creates expectation that God will move. Then, when He moves again, it builds your faith even more, which in turn creates greater expectation. It's a cycle, and the more we see God move, the more we know He can do things immeasurably greater than anything we could ever imagine. When I was a baby in my faith, there were things I never would have believed could happen. But as my faith grows, so does my belief that there is nothing too hard for the Lord.

Living a Life of Expectation

Don't be afraid to expect greater things. God promised that He "has blessed us in Christ with every spiritual blessing in the heavenly places" (Eph. 1:3). God promised "that he who began a good work in you will bring it to completion at the day of Jesus Christ" (Phil. 1:6). "No eye has seen, nor ear heard, nor the heart of man imagined, what God has prepared for those who love him" (1 Cor. 2:9).

TRUST IN THE LORD

Living a life of expectation starts with trusting the Lord. Proverbs 3:5–6 says, "Trust in the LORD with all your heart, and lean not on your own understanding; in all your ways acknowledge Him, and He shall direct your paths" (NKJV).

You know whom you trust by looking at who you go to first when you have an issue. When a storm hits your life, is your initial reaction to post about it on social media? Do you text half a dozen of your closest friends to whine and complain? Do you call your mom for some advice? Or do you pray? Do you turn to the One who can calm even the fiercest storm?

So many times, you end up with all kinds of frustrations, all kinds of troubles, all kinds of worries, and all kinds of problems because you aren't placing your trust where you should. You get all bent out of shape because God is not doing it the way you want to do it. You think things should be working out according to your plan and that God is just along for the ride. That is trusting in your flesh, in yourself, rather than trusting the Lord.

Proverbs 3:5 says to trust the Lord with all your heart. That means that with the core of your being, with everything in you, with all your soul, with all your strength, with all your mind, and with all your heart, you choose to trust God. Trust is kind of like when you go home after church and decide to take a nap. When you climb into your bed, you put all your weight on it without thinking twice. If you're tired enough, you may even completely flop onto your bed. You trust the bed to hold your weight. You don't go home, walk into your bedroom, and give the mattress a few firm pushes to see what happens. You don't kneel on the bed with one leg and wait a few seconds to see if collapse is imminent. You just trust the bed will hold you up. So the question is, Do you trust the bed more than you do God?

Do you trust God to hold you up? Do you lean on God? Do you trust Him so much that you can pray, "Lord, You know that something's going on with me, but I'm going to trust You"?

Do you trust God? Or do you lean on your own understanding? Look at what the verse is saying. Let me tell it to you straight: Leaning on your own understanding will jack you up. When you lean on your own understanding, you are making everything about you. Then your pride makes an appearance, and you know by now that when you are walking in pride, you are being counseled by the enemy.

"In all your ways acknowledge Him..." *Merriam-Webster* defines *acknowledge* as "to recognize the rights, authority, or status of; to take notice of; to recognize as genuine or valid."[1] All those definitions work in this context, but what the Hebrew word for *acknowledge* means at the most basic level is "to know."[2] Oh, that is so good. Chew on that for a moment; meditate on it. In all your ways, in everything you do in life, *know Him*. This whole thing is about knowing Him. It is about being made in His image, to give Him glory, so that when people see

Living a Life of Expectation

you—even though they see your personality and your characteristics—they see Jesus in you.

Knowing Jesus also connects to trusting Him. How much do you trust a complete stranger? How much do you trust a casual acquaintance? How does that compare with how much you trust the people you have spent lots of time with and know really well? The more you get to know Jesus and the more you get to know His ways and the more you get to know His heart, the easier it is to trust Him.

"In all your ways acknowledge Him, and He shall direct your paths." We all have taken a wrong turn or two. We all have gotten lost or turned around. But when you trust the Lord, you can trust Him to get you back on the right path—or even get someone else back on the right path.

One time when we were doing Night Out with Jesus, we were at a gas station. There was a young guy standing next to his car, and we went to pay for his gas. While his tank was filling up, we had a conversation with him. We didn't know him or anything about his story, but he had left his home in Chicago two days earlier after a fight with his father. He stopped at a gas station in Houston, and that's when a team of us from our church went up to him, paid for his gas, and started telling him things about himself that we had no way of knowing—that is, no way of knowing without the Holy Spirit speaking to our hearts. The guy started to cry. He knew that something supernatural was happening, that God was reaching out to him, trying to get him back on the right path.

The following Monday, we got a phone call at the church. It was the guy's dad, calling from Chicago. The dad was a believer. He was crying as he told us his story. He told us his son had gotten really mad at him and had said that he didn't want anything to do with God anymore. He was done with "God stuff." The son got in his car and took off.

His son then stopped at the gas station where a bunch of God people started talking to him about God stuff. There was no way the son could argue that God had not intervened, because the people who talked to him knew things they could not have known without God. So the son called his dad, crying, and repented.

The dad thanked us again and again. He told us he had been praying, and he said, "I've been believing for my son's salvation, but he left. I was asking God to do a miracle in his life. And I didn't know how He was going to do it."

The son was on the wrong path. The dad trusted God and prayed. And there was a miracle. It was a powerful confirmation for us as a church and as individuals that living a life of expectation sets the stage for the miraculous. Expectation isn't passive hopefulness; it's active faith. Having expectation requires a shift in your mindset from wondering if God might move to confidently trusting that He will.

Remember the widow who was in so much debt that her children were going to be taken as slaves? All she had was one jar of oil, but when Elisha told her, "Go outside, borrow vessels from all your neighbors, empty vessels and not too few," the widow had an expectation of provision (2 Kings 4:3). Her expectation led to a miracle of multiplication. God multiplied that oil so much that the widow could pay off all her debts and still have money to live on.

Another Bible story about expectation is when Peter was in prison. This story is funny. When Peter was thrown in jail, "earnest prayer for him was made to God by the church" (Acts 12:5). The early church prayed fervently. They prayed in expectation that God would intervene

Living a Life of Expectation

in the situation and rescue Peter. And that's exactly what God did. Peter was asleep in the prison, chained up between two soldiers. An angel showed up, woke up Peter, and told him to get up. The chains just fell from his hands. He followed the angel out of the prison, walking right past two sentries. When they got to the gate leading out into the city, the gate just opened, and Peter walked right through it into freedom.

Here's the funny part: Peter knew that the church was praying for him, so he went to the house where he knew they would be gathered.

> And when he knocked at the door of the gateway, a servant girl named Rhoda came to answer. Recognizing Peter's voice, in her joy she did not open the gate but ran in and reported that Peter was standing at the gate. They said to her, "You are out of your mind." But she kept insisting that it was so, and they kept saying, "It is his angel!" But Peter continued knocking, and when they opened, they saw him and were amazed.
>
> —ACTS 12:13–16

The church expected God to move, but God definitely didn't move the way they expected. Rhoda was so surprised she didn't even let Peter in, leaving him standing outside, still knocking on the door. And the other church members thought Rhoda was crazy!

I love that even though they were living in expectation, they were still surprised. I live in expectation, and I love it when I get surprised. I hope I never lose the wonder that the miraculous inspires.

In Christ

Part of living in expectation and trusting the Lord is understanding who you are in Christ. I feel like so many of the crises we face today are rooted in the fact that so many people are having an identity crisis. They don't understand who they are in Christ. That's one of the reasons I love the Book of Ephesians. It uses the phrase *in Christ* over and over and over again as it establishes just who we are in Christ.

Ephesians 1:3–7 (NKJV) says,

> Blessed be the God and Father of our Lord Jesus Christ, who has blessed us with every spiritual blessing in the heavenly places in Christ, just as He chose us in Him before the foundation of the world, that we should be holy and without blame before Him in love, having predestined us to adoption as sons by Jesus Christ to Himself, according to the good pleasure of His will, to the praise of the glory of His grace, by which He made us accepted in the Beloved. In Him we have redemption through His blood, the forgiveness of sins, according to the riches of His grace.

Just those few verses tell us that in Christ we are blessed, chosen, holy, blameless, loved, adopted, accepted, redeemed, and forgiven. Wow!

Knowing who you are in Christ is so powerful. When the enemy goes on the attack with his lies, knowing who you are in Christ helps you fight back. For example, if the enemy attacks you with rejection, you can say, "Nope! I'm not rejected. I have been chosen and accepted, and God adopted me into His family."

Living a Life of Expectation

If you read a little further in Ephesians 1, you will see that you were also "sealed with the promised Holy Spirit" (v. 13, CSB). Combined with the other verses, this means you were chosen by the Father, you were redeemed by the Son, and you were sealed by the Holy Spirit. That paints such a beautiful picture of who you are. God the Father chose you specifically to be His child. He created you, He loves you, and He says, "I have called you by name, you are mine" (Isa. 43:1). Then Jesus, the Son of God, redeemed you. That means He paid the ransom for you. You were held captive by sin, but Jesus paid the ultimate price for your freedom. Then the Holy Spirit sealed you. He put His mark on you to make it clear that you belong to Him, and there is nothing the enemy can do about that.

I think if you really understood what it means to be a child of God, you might be living differently. You might be trusting God more. You might be living in greater expectation of what your heavenly Father will do in your life.

When I'm doing marriage mediation, one of the most important parts is in the beginning when I start asking them questions about where their identity lies. Is it in work? Is it in your family? Is it in this? Is it in that? They generally give the spiritual answer they think I want to hear: "My identity is in Christ."

A couple of pages later, the questions are phrased differently but still reveal where their identity lies. For example, I ask, "What makes you feel secure? What makes you feel the most safe?" I will get a different answer then. And then I'll say, "Wait a minute. When I asked you about your identity, you said it was in Christ. But when I asked you what makes you feel the most safe, you said something else. You didn't mention Jesus at all."

The discrepancy in their answers tells me a lot about their hearts and where their identity truly lies. I hear what they are saying with their lips—giving me the spiritual answer they think I want to hear—but the truth is that their hearts are not rooted and grounded in the love of Christ.

The apostle Paul wrote, "You, being rooted and grounded in love, may have strength to comprehend with all the saints what is the breadth and length and height and depth, and to know the love of Christ that surpasses knowledge, that you may be filled with all the fullness of God" (Eph. 3:17–19).

When you don't understand who you are in Christ, you don't understand what it actually means to be loved by Him. You don't understand "the breadth and length and height and depth" of His love. You don't understand that His love is enough to cover all your sin. You don't understand there is nothing that could ever separate you from His love. You don't understand that He wants you to abide in His love. You don't understand that His love is unfailing and everlasting.

Your true identity is not in your job or your family or your friends or your gifts or anything other than Jesus. I think placing your identity in something temporal is why many people's lives fall apart. If your identity is in your job but then you lose your job, what happens then? If your identity is in your friends but then all of a sudden your friends aren't there anymore, what happens to your identity?

Don't get me wrong. Your job, your family, your friends, your gifts, and other things like that are part of your identity; they are part of who you are. But the foundation of your identity—the place where your acceptance, your security, and your purpose are rooted—is in Christ. When who you are in Christ is the basis of your identity, if everything else falls apart, you still have a foundation. Your identity won't be turned to rubble. You will have a foundation you can build on.

Remember, all these things come from an authentic, intimate relationship with God. God begins by sharing with us who we are. He wants us to know who we really are because what we do grows out of who we are. We don't do in order to become. We become in order to do. When you get saved, when you become a follower of Jesus, you become a new person in Christ. You get adopted into God's family so that you can do all the things He made you to do. God made you for a specific purpose. In fact, God made you a masterpiece so you can fulfill that specific purpose: "For we are God's masterpiece. He has created us anew in Christ Jesus, so we can do the good things he planned for us long ago" (Eph. 2:10, NLT).

The more you understand who you are, the more you will trust the Lord. The more you understand what it means to be a son or daughter of the Most High, the more you will expect God to move. When you are in an authentic, heart-level relationship with Jesus, you will understand that He "is able to do immeasurably more than all we ask or imagine, according to his power that is at work within us" (Eph. 3:20, NIV).

AUTHENTIC RELATIONSHIP

I keep using the term *authentic relationship* in this book because, ultimately, experiencing the miraculous in your life springs from an authentic relationship with God.

Many believers today have head knowledge about God, but they never truly experience Him or encounter Him in a way that transforms their lives. What's in their heads never makes it to their hearts. I think most people have facts about God, and I've noticed how easy it is to spend a lot of time arguing over facts about God rather than actually getting to know Him. If you look at the apostle Paul's prayers for the Ephesian believers, you will see he didn't want them to learn more facts about God—he wanted them to truly know the Lord in a deep and life-changing way:

> I do not cease to give thanks for you, remembering you in my prayers, that the God of our Lord Jesus Christ, the Father of glory, may give you the Spirit of *wisdom* and of *revelation* in the *knowledge* of him, having the eyes of your hearts *enlightened*, that you may *know* what is the hope to which he has called you, what are the riches of his glorious inheritance in the saints, and what is the immeasurable greatness of his power toward us who believe, according to the working of his great might that he worked in Christ when he raised him from the dead and seated him at his right hand in the heavenly places, far above all rule and authority and power and dominion, and above every name that is named, not only in this age but also in the one to come.
> —EPHESIANS 1:16–21, EMPHASIS ADDED

For this reason I bow my knees before the Father, from whom every family in heaven and on earth is named, that according to the riches of his glory he may grant you to be strengthened with power through his Spirit in your inner being, so that Christ may dwell in your hearts through faith—that you, being rooted and grounded in love, may have strength to *comprehend* with all the saints what is

Living a Life of Expectation

> the breadth and length and height and depth, and
> to *know* the love of Christ that surpasses knowledge,
> that you may be filled with all the fullness of God.
> —Ephesians 3:14–19, emphasis added

This planet is full of people who have theoretical knowledge of God but lack the experience of Him. In other words, they have a form of godliness yet deny the power thereof (2 Tim. 3:5). They can spout facts about God, but they really don't know God.

When Jesus chose the twelve disciples, He called them to do something before He sent them out to preach and cast out demons. He called them to be with Him:

> And he went up on the mountain and called to him those whom he desired, and they came to him. And he appointed twelve (whom he also named apostles) *so that they might be with him* and he might send them out to preach and have authority to cast out demons.
> —Mark 3:13–15, emphasis added

No matter the calling the Lord has for your life—pastor, apostle, evangelist, teacher, prophet, father, mother, friend, mentor, doctor, lawyer, butcher, baker, candlestick maker—your primary calling is to be with Jesus. Your primary calling is to get to know Jesus by developing an authentic relationship with Him. That's what the Lord wants. That's what He longs for. As I said earlier, He doesn't want a casual, surface-level relationship with you, as if you were just an acquaintance. He doesn't want a Sunday-morning-only relationship. He wants a deep, authentic, intimate, heart-level, everyday relationship with you.

Whatever your calling is, if you don't know Jesus, you have no power to do it the way God has called you to. There are many things you can do without Jesus, and many of those things can be done well without Him—but if you truly want to fulfill your God-given purpose, if you truly want to walk in the calling that God has placed on your life, you need the power that comes from a relationship with Jesus.

When people pursue their callings without power, it often creates chaos—there is more hurt than healing, there is more panic than peace, there is more venom than victory, there is more sorrow than salvation, and there is more fear than faith.

There is no power, no hope, no freedom, and no joy without a close, intimate relationship with Jesus. You have to be plugged into the power source. You have to be connected to Him. That's how you're going to fulfill your calling. That's how you are going to passionately pursue your purpose. That is how you are going to help other people. That is how you are going to build the kingdom. That is how you are going to have abundant life. That is how you are going to grow in Him. That is how you are going to experience the supernatural.

When you have a relationship with God, He is not trying to just transfer information. His purpose is transformation. When you delight in the Lord, your heart starts to line up with heaven.

As a follower of Jesus, as part of the body of Christ, you are in partnership with God. You are in partnership with His Word. You are in partnership with the Holy Spirit to fulfill the plans and purposes for your life. So whenever the way seems crooked on your current endeavor, whenever you lose your way, whenever you notice you are veering off the path, you need to check your alignment.

- Are you out of alignment with your *partnership*? Are you out of alignment with the Word or what the Holy Spirit has been telling you?

- Are you out of alignment in *prioritizing* your relationship with Jesus? Are you putting what Jesus wants first in your endeavor?

- Are you out of alignment in your *pursuit* of Jesus? (Do you remember that question about chasing miracles instead of chasing Jesus?)

- Are you out of alignment in *purity*? Are you pure in heart? When God speaks to you and it isn't what you want or expect, do you throw a temper tantrum, or do you humbly submit to His will?

Check your alignment, and stay connected. Remain in the vine so you bear a bumper crop of good fruit.

Second Peter 3:18 says, "Grow in the grace and knowledge of our Lord and Savior Jesus Christ." Isn't that an amazing truth, that we can grow in the grace and knowledge of Jesus? The question is, Are you still growing in God?

First Peter 2:2 says, "Like newborn infants, desire the pure milk of the word, so that by it you may grow up into your salvation" (CSB). Babies desire milk. They long for it. They need it. And when they consume it, it helps them grow. Are you like that with the Word of God? Do you desire it? Do you long for it? Do you need it? Do you consume it so it helps you grow?

Luke 10:38–42 (CSB) tells a story about Mary and Martha, the sisters of Lazarus and friends of Jesus:

> While they were traveling, he entered a village, and a woman named Martha welcomed him into her home. She had a sister named Mary, who also sat at the Lord's feet and was listening to what he said. But Martha was distracted by her many tasks, and she came up and asked, "Lord, don't you care that my sister has left me to serve alone? So tell her to give me a hand."
>
> The Lord answered her, "Martha, Martha, you are worried and upset about many things, but one thing is necessary. Mary has made the right choice, and it will not be taken away from her."

The story of Mary and Martha shows the importance of prioritizing your relationship with God over your performance for Him. When Mary sat at the feet of Jesus, she was in a posture of a student being taught by the Master. It was a posture of humility. It also demonstrated she was hungry for the Word. Mary let the busyness of life and the to-do lists and the chores and all the other distractions fall to the wayside so she could sit at Jesus' feet, listening to His words, learning from Him, and being transformed in the presence of God. And even though there were things that needed to be done in her household, Jesus said Mary made the right choice. God desires to have fellowship with us. He wants to spend time with us. He wants to teach us and transform us.

When I went to write one of my books, I made it about me. Day one, I locked myself in a room. I had Ruthy

Living a Life of Expectation

bring me a sweater because I decided I wasn't comfortable enough to write. I had my water, my books, and everything I needed to write, and I said, "OK, Lord, let's go." And then I noticed the flow I had with the Holy Spirit was gone. So I went to the Lord and said, "Man, God, we got to write this."

God said, "Whoa, wait a minute. I want to spend time with you."

Do you know how I know I had made it about me? When God told me to stop and spend time with Him, my response was, "Yeah, God, but I have a deadline, and I have this contract..." I told God about all the stuff I had going on—like He didn't know.

He asked, "What if you missed the deadline? What if you missed out on publishing the book?"

I tried reasoning with God about responsibility and some other things.

Then God said, "If you're talking to Me and you miss the deadline, I'm good with that."

So I spent the day with the Lord.

Day two started off better because I had postured my heart the way I was supposed to. God said He wanted to spend the day with me again. So that's what we did. And God tested me later that day by telling me to go write. I started writing, and I had only written a tiny bit when God said, "Done!"

I then went to worship the Lord on Sunday, and God downloaded a bunch of stuff to me. He could have given me all of it the previous two days, but God moves when He wants to and how He wants to. I had been letting my flesh get in the way, and God checked me. He moved me back to the place where it was about Him, not about me.

That's the kind of thing that God does when you are in an authentic relationship with Him.

Jesus wants authentic relationship. He wants your heart. Religious behavior and posturing do not please Him, nor do they move His heart.

It's all about Jesus. When you are in an authentic relationship with Him, you understand that God's ways are not our ways. You chase Jesus, not miracles—although miracles happen when you are chasing Jesus. Your perspective is changed, so you can see the supernatural in both the big things and the little things. You live in the power and authority of the Spirit. You worship in spirit and truth, and your life is full of both the Word of God and the Holy Spirit.

Even in the wilderness you know that man does not live by bread alone. You walk by faith, not by sight, even when it seems crazy, and your faith pleases God. You know that faith the size of a mustard seed is enough to produce supernatural results. You are continually washed by the water of the Word, and you are being transformed into His image, from glory to glory. You talk to God like a Father, like a friend. You bear good fruit. You trust Him. You love Him. You are His, and He is yours. When you are in an authentic relationship with Jesus, crazy stuff happens all the time—but you know the truth. Those things aren't crazy. They are the work of God.

The impossible of God, the thing that requires crazy faith from you, can be an opportunity to allow God to do a new thing in you, to make a way in your wilderness, to provide a stream in your wasteland. You have been restored to a relationship in right standing with almighty God, the Creator of the universe, through the

Living a Life of Expectation

death and resurrection of Jesus. Jesus paid your ransom. He redeemed you. But your redemption isn't an end in itself. It is an opportunity! God wants to use you in crazy ways if you are willing to trust Him and step out in faith.

Trust the Lord. Walk by faith. Live in expectation. God desires to show up more than we even want Him to. When you live a life of expectation, it transforms your life. It changes routine trips to the grocery store, conversations at your job, and mundane family dinners into potential divine encounters. Life is full of surprises when you expect the supernatural and have eyes to see it when it happens.

When we expect God to move, He moves. It happens all the time when we're willing to take Him at His Word, when we're willing to posture our hearts in worship and obedience. When He moves, it may not look like what we expected. But it is still God. He responds to expectation. When we have that intimate relationship with Him, we will recognize His leading. We will recognize His voice. We will recognize the move of His Spirit, and we will walk by faith, stepping out of our comfort zones and daring to believe that God will back us up. Supernatural experiences start with humility and a step of faith.

Expectation is not passive. It's active. That means I am going to be training my brain to operate in faith by reading God's Word, writing His Word on my heart, speaking words of life, speaking the truth, and reminding God of His promises. I am going to cultivate expectation by being sensitive to the leading of the Holy Spirit. I am going to listen for the still, small voice of the Lord. I'm going to listen for the voice behind me saying, "This is the way. Walk in it."

As you are living this life of expectation, you will see God move in miraculous ways. And you should share the stories of the ways you see God move with others. You should share stories of His faithfulness, His goodness, His kindness, His mercy, His grace, His provision, His power, His presence, and His peace. When you share those stories, it creates more expectation in your heart and in the hearts of others. When you testify about moments you witnessed God move, faith arises in you and in others. Faith fuels expectation, and expectation fuels faith. Expectation reveals God's heart, and expectation is definitely contagious. And as faith and expectation continue to grow and fuel each other, you create a community where miracles are commonplace.

Remember that supernatural encounters are not just rewards for perfect people with a perfect spiritual life. Supernatural, miraculous acts are expressions of God's extravagant love. They are demonstrations of His abounding grace that are available to every single person who is willing to trust Him. When you commit to living expectantly, you'll be amazed at how naturally the supernatural unfolds.

Do what God is telling you to do. He is always inviting you into authentic relationship with Him. He is saying, "Come!" And when you accept the invitation, you step into the supernatural. Live with your eyes wide open, your heart ready, and your spirit eager to do what God wants to do today. Then watch how quickly you end up seeing the fingerprints of God. There will be some people who still say that the supernatural, the miraculous, and the impossible things that happen in your life are just coincidences or happened by chance, but you will know the truth. When you share your testimonies of the miraculous, there will be people that say, "That's crazy!" But for those of us who know Jesus and thus know the truth, we'll shout joyfully, "That's not crazy. That's God!"

Chapter 10
SUPERNATURAL SALVATION

You've made it to the end of this book—and if you've been reading closely, you've probably had at least a few moments when you thought, "That's wild! That's crazy! No, that's God!"

But now it gets real. It gets personal. I want to talk to you about the craziest, most supernatural thing God can do in a person's life. It's not physical healing. It's not an encounter with an angel. It's not a financial breakthrough.

The most miraculous thing that could ever occur in your life is your eternal salvation.

Listen up, because salvation is the first step—one that can't be skipped over—if you want to get to know the Creator of the universe, if you want to get to know Jesus, and if you truly want to experience the supernatural in your life. If you miss this part, you might enjoy some God moments, but you will never actually know Him. And I don't want that for you. More importantly, God doesn't want that for you.

You may be wondering, "How can I know for sure if I'm saved?" If that's you, this chapter is for you. Let's take a look at what it means to be saved, not based on feelings or opinions or traditions but based on the Word of God.

WHAT IS SALVATION?

The Bible tells us salvation isn't about being a good person. It's not about going to church, saying a prayer once, or believing in God in your head.

The Greek word for *saved* in the New Testament is *sōzō*—which means to be made whole and to be delivered, rescued, and healed.[1] Salvation is not just a ticket to heaven. It's a complete transformation that starts now. It's a complete rebirth. Jesus gives you a new identity in Him. You are rescued from death to life. "Therefore, if anyone is in Christ, he is a new creation. The old has passed away; behold, the new has come" (2 Cor. 5:17).

Romans 10:9–10 tells you how to receive salvation, how to get saved:

> If you confess with your mouth that Jesus is Lord and believe in your heart that God raised him from the dead, you will be saved. For with the heart one believes and is justified, and with the mouth one confesses and is saved.

This kind of belief is more than just acknowledging something in your mind. Biblically, *believe* means to trust, to have faith in, to be persuaded of, to commit to.[2] Belief isn't just about the words that come out of your mouth or the thoughts in your mind. It's about what you accept as true way down deep in your heart.

As I mentioned earlier, I think the issue some people have is that they confess with their mouths, but they don't believe with their hearts. They try to convince themselves to believe in their minds, but they don't recognize that it is a heart issue. Belief starts in your heart.

And when you have that belief, that acceptance in your heart, it means that Jesus becomes Lord of your life, not just the Savior you call on when life is hard. You no longer run your life—He does. You choose to submit to His authority, His Word, His will, and His way.

That's salvation. And that is supernatural.

What It Looks Like If You're Truly Saved

Let's make this practical. Because real faith produces real fruit.

You won't be perfect—no one other than Jesus is—but when you've really surrendered to Jesus, things start to shift. You start to change because Christ is now living inside you (Gal. 2:20). Your body becomes a temple of the Holy Spirit (1 Cor. 3:16; 6:19), and the Spirit starts to change you into the image of Christ, from glory to glory (2 Cor. 3:18).

Here's what that change usually looks like:

- **Your desires change.** You want to follow Jesus. Sin starts to feel uncomfortable, not exciting. You have a hunger for the Word, prayer, and being around other believers.

- **You practice repentance.** You don't hide sin anymore—you bring it into the light. You may still stumble, but your direction is toward Jesus, not away from Him. Conviction draws you closer to God, not into shame.

- **Obedience becomes normal.** You start obeying God, even when it's inconvenient. You forgive people. You give generously. You walk away from gossip and compromise. You start doing things His way, not yours.

- **You're planted in a community of believers.** You're not just attending church—you're becoming the church. You serve, you grow, you get sharpened by others, and you're accountable.

- **You bear fruit.** You bear good fruit, real fruit, the fruit of the Spirit: "love, joy, peace, patience, kindness, goodness, faithfulness, gentleness, self-control" (Gal. 5:22–23). People around you notice: "You're different." That's because Jesus said, "You will recognize them by their fruits" (Matt. 7:16).

WHAT IT LOOKS LIKE IF YOU'RE *NOT* FOLLOWING JESUS

Some people said a prayer once, but nothing ever changed. Others think they're good with God, but they're just living life on their own terms. There is no fruit. There is no change. They don't look more and more like Jesus; they look more and more like the world. Jesus said, "Why do you call me 'Lord, Lord,' and not do what I tell you?" (Luke 6:46). When you truly get saved and make Jesus the Lord of your life, it isn't just lip service. Your life should show the fruit of your belief.

Here are some signs you may not truly be saved:

- **You have no conviction about sin.** You sin and don't care. You justify behavior the Bible clearly says is wrong.

- **You don't have a hunger for God.** You rarely (or never) pray, read the Word, or want to grow in your faith.

- **You live for yourself.** Jesus isn't Lord—you are. Decisions, relationships, finances—it's all your way, not His.

- **You have no community and no accountability.** You avoid church, hide from Christian friendships, or treat your faith as private.

- **You don't bear fruit, even after a long time has passed.** No one expects you to have the Christian life down pat overnight. But if you look exactly the same now as you did years ago, with no spiritual growth and no transformation, then you aren't bearing good fruit.

Let's be honest: You can go to church and still be lost. You can believe in Jesus and still not follow Him. You can say all the right things without ever having your heart changed.

That's why this chapter matters.

Picture this. You're standing in a courtroom. You've been living as a spiritual orphan, doing life your way. And now the judge stands before you, holding adoption papers covered in the blood of Jesus.

He says, "These papers are paid for. You don't need to

earn your spot. You just need to say yes. Do you want to come home?"

That's salvation. It's God inviting you to join His family. It's not religion—it's relationship.

It's not about what you can do for God—it's about what He already did for you. God has already chosen you to be His child. All you have to do is accept it in your heart.

This Is Your Moment

Ask yourself these four questions honestly:

1. Is Jesus truly Lord of my life—or is Jesus just a name I say?
2. If I died today, do I have peace knowing I'm saved—not because I'm good but because Jesus is good?
3. Have I seen real change in my desires, actions, and direction?
4. Am I following Him daily, or just when it's convenient?

If those questions shake you—good. That means the Holy Spirit is moving in you.

If you've never fully surrendered your life to Jesus—or if you're unsure you ever really have—this is your moment. This isn't the moment for an emotional decision, but rather a spiritual surrender to the One who loves you and gave His life for you so that you could be called a child of God.

Pray something like this from your heart:

Supernatural Salvation

> *Jesus, I believe You are the Son of God. I believe You died for my sins and rose again. I confess You as my Lord and Savior. I don't want to live my way anymore—I want to follow You. Forgive me. Change me. Fill me with Your Spirit. I surrender. In Jesus' name, amen.*

If you prayed that and meant it, you didn't just say a prayer—you entered a new life. You were born again. You're saved.

Now that you're saved, it's time to begin your discipleship journey, where you grow in faith and become more and more like Jesus, where you are washed in the water of the Word, where you are empowered by the Holy Spirit, where you live a life of expectation, and where you see the supernatural.

Salvation is the starting line, not the finish line. Here's what to do next:

- **Get baptized.** It's your public declaration that you've died to your old life and been raised with Christ (Rom. 6:4).

- **Start reading the Bible daily.** Begin with the Gospel of John or Mark. Ask the Holy Spirit to help you understand.

- **Join a church or faith community.** You grow best around others who love Jesus and can help you stay strong.

- **Pray often and honestly.** Prayer is just talking with your Father. Keep it real.

- **Share your story.** Tell someone about what Jesus did for you, how He changed you. Share how you have seen the supernatural hand of God at work in your life. Your testimony is powerful.

If you made that decision today, that isn't crazy—no, that's God.

Heaven is rejoicing (Luke 15:7), and your new life has begun. You're no longer who you were. You're a child of God. And this is just the beginning.

Please contact pray4me@charismamedia.com so my publisher can send you some materials that will help you become established in your relationship with the Lord. If you want to know the next steps or need help finding a church or discipleship group, scan this QR code:

Let's go. Let's grow. Let's live lives that make people say, "That's crazy—no, that's God!"

NOTES

CHAPTER 1
1. Merriam-Webster, "worship," accessed May 5, 2025, https://www.merriam-webster.com/dictionary/worship.
2. Blue Letter Bible, "šāḥâ," accessed May 5, 2025, https://www.blueletterbible.org/lexicon/h7812/kjv/wlc/0-1/.
3. Blue Letter Bible, "proskyneō," accessed May 6, 2025, https://www.blueletterbible.org/lexicon/g4352/kjv/tr/0-1/.

CHAPTER 4
1. This Is Real with Juan Martinez, "GW12—the Panel (8:45 a.m. Service)," YouTube, March 3, 2025, https://www.youtube.com/watch?v=N60p9WvGCuw.
2. Kelly Kane Lewis, "The Wheelchair Was My Future, God Had Other Plans," The Christian Broadcasting Network, accessed May 16, 2025, https://cbn.com/article/prayer/wheelchair-was-my-future-god-had-other-plans.

CHAPTER 5
1. Blue Letter Bible, "pistis," accessed May 16, 2025, https://www.blueletterbible.org/lexicon/g4102/kjv/tr/0-1/.
2. LanGeek Dictionary, "Impossible," accessed May 19, 2025, https://dictionary.langeek.co/en/word/94300?entry=impossible.

CHAPTER 6
1. Blue Letter Bible, "hodos," accessed May 19, 2025, https://www.blueletterbible.org/lexicon/g3598/kjv/tr/0-1/.

CHAPTER 7

1. Edward McKendree Bounds, *The Classic Collection on Prayer* (Bridge-Logos Publishers, 2001), 79.

CHAPTER 8

1. Blue Letter Bible, "*menō*," accessed May 21, 2025, https://www.blueletterbible.org/lexicon/g3306/kjv/tr/0-1/.
2. Blue Letter Bible, "*qāḏaš*," accessed May 21, 2025, https://www.blueletterbible.org/lexicon/h6942/kjv/wlc/0-1/.
3. Blue Letter Bible, "*pāra'*," accessed May 21, 2025, https://www.blueletterbible.org/lexicon/h6544/kjv/wlc/0-1/.

CHAPTER 9

1. *Merriam-Webster*, "acknowledge," accessed May 21, 2025, https://www.merriam-webster.com/dictionary/acknowledge.
2. Blue Letter Bible, "*yāḏa'*," accessed May 21, 2025, https://www.blueletterbible.org/lexicon/h3045/kjv/wlc/0-1/.

CHAPTER 10

1. Blue Letter Bible, "*sōzō*," accessed May 21, 2025, https://www.blueletterbible.org/lexicon/g4982/kjv/tr/0-1/.
2. Blue Letter Bible, "*pisteuō*," accessed May 21, 2025, https://www.blueletterbible.org/lexicon/g4100/kjv/tr/0-1/.

ACKNOWLEDGMENTS

*F*IRST AND FOREVER, *thank You, Jesus.* You rescued me, restored me, rewrote my story, and then handed me the pen. Without You, I wouldn't be alive—let alone an author. This book is for Your glory, and I know we're only getting started.

To my beautiful wife, *Ruthy*, my Baby Ruth—you've stood by my side with unshakable love and relentless support. You've believed in the call on my life when others couldn't see it. Thank you for being my partner in life, faith, and every "crazy" God adventure.

To my kids—*Jonathan, Valery, Nina, Josh, Jay, and Johnathan*—you are my joy. *Jonathan*, your strength inspires me. And *Nina*, your willingness to jump in headfirst by faith, especially in the hard seasons, humbles me. Thank you for running with me.

To my *older brother, John Ramirez*—thank you for always believing in me and reminding me of the warrior that God called me to be.

To *Charisma House* and everyone involved in publishing this message—thank you for giving voice to the supernatural.

To every *editor, encourager, and behind-the-scenes helper*—I see you, and God sees you.

To my friends and family in the faith—*Angel and*

Marianna, James and Megan, Henry and Liz, Vinny and Sara, Gregg and Michelle, G and Krystal, April, and my amazing daughter-in-law, Stephanie—your prayers, encouragement, and presence mean more than you know.

To the *pastoral staff at Get Wrapped Church* and the whole *Get Wrapped family*—you have been a fortress of support and love. I am honored to walk this journey with you.

To *every pastor and church* that welcomed me, poured into me, and believed in the vision, even when it sounded crazy—thank you. *David Vestal* and *Don Babin*, thank you for being true friends.

And finally, to *every pastor, mentor, and spiritual leader* who ever spoke a word of life into me—you know who you are. Thank you for being part of this story.

This book is proof that God still does the impossible—and when people say, "That's crazy," I'll keep responding, "No, that's God."

ABOUT THE AUTHOR

Juan Martinez serves as the senior pastor of Get Wrapped Church in Spring, Texas, and the founder of Love Live Lead Ministry. Since 2010 the ministry has seen thousands of people say yes to Christ. His "heartbeat" and main focus is simply winning souls by wrapping them in the love of Christ. A true revivalist, Martinez has a burning passion to see the lost saved, the broken mended, the afflicted healed, and the body of Christ operating in its God-given authority. He speaks at conferences throughout the nation and also partners in outreaches around the United States. He has appeared on many televised programs, including Trinity Broadcasting Network (TBN), TBN Salsa, CTN Vegas, JDM, *The Jim Bakker Show*, and *The Mondo Show*, and hosts a radio show and podcast called *This Is REAL*.

Martinez is the author of *Beyond the Yellow Brick Road* and *Prison Break*, and coauthor of *Imperfect Dads, One Perfect Father*. God has transformed him from having a "kill, steal, and destroy" mentality to a seed-sowing mindset, spreading the good news to all who will listen. He has seen God move miraculously in his life and longs to hear the world say, "That's crazy," as we shout, "No, that's God!"

Martinez lives in Houston with his wife, Ruthy (his Baby Ruth). They have six children: Jonathan, Josh, Valery, Johnathan, Jay, and Janina.

To learn more about Juan Martinez's ministry or to buy merchandise, visit

www.JuanMartinez.tv
www.Getwrapped.tv
www.heavicans.com